ESSENTIAL DRAMATURGY

Essential Dramaturgy: The Mindset and Skillset provides a concrete way to approach the work of a dramaturg. It explores ways to refine the process of defining, evaluating, and communicating that is essential to effective dramaturgical work. It then looks at how this outlook enhances the practical skills of production and new play dramaturgy. The book explains what a dramaturg does, what the role can be, and how best to refine and teach the skillset and mindset.

Theresa Lang is a teacher, director, and dramaturg. She holds a BA in Drama from the University of Dallas, an MA in Theatre from Brown University, and a PhD in Drama from Tufts University. A theatre historian, her areas of specialty include popular entertainment, the censorship of urban space, and the development of the American theatre. As a practitioner she is particularly interested in the development and production of new work and under-represented voices. She is the dramaturg of Come on Over Ensemble Theatre and is on the faculty at the Boston Conservatory at Berklee and at Boston College. Theresa is the Chair of Dramaturgy and the Coordinator of Devised Theatre for Region 1 of the Kennedy Center American College Theatre Festival, and was the Associate Director of the inaugural New Play Dramaturgy Intensive at the Kennedy Center.

ESSENTIAL DRAMATURGY

THE MINDSET AND SKILLSET

Theresa Lang

Routledge
Taylor & Francis Group

NEW YORK AND LONDON

First published 2017
by Routledge
711 Third Avenue, New York, NY 10017

and by Routledge
2 Park Square, Milton Park, Abingdon, Oxon OX14 4RN

Routledge is an imprint of the Taylor & Francis Group, an informa business

© 2017 Taylor & Francis

Library of Congress Cataloging in Publication Data
Names: Lang, Theresa, author.
Title: Essential dramaturgy : the mindset and skillset / Theresa Lang.
Description: New York : Routledge/Taylor & Francis Group, 2017. |
    Includes bibliographical references and index.
Identifiers: LCCN 2016035346 | ISBN 9781138902176 (hbk : alk. paper) |
    ISBN 9781138902152 (pbk : alk. paper) | ISBN 9781315697604
    (ebk : alk. paper)
Subjects: LCSH: Theater—Production and direction. | Dramaturges.
Classification: LCC PN2053 .L355 2017 | DDC 792.02/3—dc23

ISBN: 978-1-138-90217-6 (hbk)
ISBN: 978-1-138-90215-2 (pbk)
ISBN: 978-1-315-69760-4 (ebk)

Typeset in Bembo
by Swales & Willis Ltd, Exeter, Devon, UK

This book is dedicated to the student dramaturgs
who began their first show by googling
what a dramaturg does.

CONTENTS

Foreword by Anne G. Morgan   viii
Acknowledgments   xi

PART I
Mindset   **1**

1 **From Noun to Verb**   3

2 **Questions Asked and Answered**   13

3 **The Forest and the Trees**   36

4 **Timing Is Everything**   56

5 **Why This, Here, Now?**   79

PART II
Skillset   **91**

6 **Dramaturg as Practice**   93

7 **The Skillset in Production**   109

8 **Dramaturgy to Enhance Audience Experience**   131

9 **Dramaturging New Plays and Devising**   153

10 **Notes from the Field**   171

Additional Resources   192
Index   194

FOREWORD

What's in a name? A defense of "dramaturg"

For as long as dramaturgy has been practiced in America, demands for a seat at the table have echoed throughout conferences, articles, and teachings. Currently, dramaturgy has become a much more accepted practice with more opportunities than ever for dramaturgs to learn and work. *Essential Dramaturgy* is a timely and robust contribution to the expanding and diversifying field. On more than one occasion, I've heard from a playwright, "I'm so excited we got this actor for the reading; he's really a tremendous dramaturg," or a director, "some of my favorite dramaturgs are designers." With dramaturgs now in some ways filling every seat at the table, the pendulum has started to swing, with the question being asked in hushed tones: "If dramaturgy is an integral part of any theater-maker's work, why do we need a specific person in the process to wear the label 'dramaturg'?"

Two recent experiences, one abroad and one here in the US, have intensified my belief in the importance of dramaturgy as a discrete discipline and the labeling of it as such. For two weeks in Latvia and Lithuania, I led university students through a series of dramaturgy workshops. Neither country's language has any word for the practice of dramaturgy. Students don't learn about it as a field, and it is not an identified professional role (this is slowly starting to shift). As if the absence of the word for what I do were not challenge enough, the English word "playwright" translates into both Latvian and Lithuanian as "dramaturg." There was much confusion around the fact that I do not write plays, and they frequently referred to me as a "technical dramaturg" and my playwright co-teacher as the "creative dramaturg." When I work with American students and theater practitioners unaccustomed to collaborating with a dramaturg, I employ as many metaphors as I can to help introduce them to my work, but I feared that my complex metaphors might not land as well in a room full of non-native English speakers.

Without a word, without a concept of the content of the workshop, without one of my tried-and-true metaphors, I found myself with something of a blank page. I had to activate, perform, and embody the concept of dramaturgy for them. I asked questions about the theatrical contexts in which they were used to learning and working. I taught them through a series of exercises, activities, examples, and conversations. And I incorporated their responses into the ongoing workshops. In short, I dramaturged. By sharing both my work and my philosophy of work, I gave them a reason to use the word.

So, after two weeks, I left my students with a new word and a concept to go with it. But words fall short, and I wonder whether the concept or the word will continue to prove useful, in my absence, given the preexisting theatrical production models in their country.

Whether in Eastern Europe, or closer to home, words are most potent when what they represent is embodied. Each spring, I interview about twenty college students for summer internships in my office. I spoke to one student this year who explained why, despite loving research and text analysis, she'd chosen to focus her studies on acting, by saying "I guess I knew what dramaturgy was but had always heard that as a career, it was intangible." What she meant was "untenable," but I had to chuckle; without a concrete product or performance at the end of a process, much of dramaturgy is indeed intangible.

The mutability and multifaceted nature of dramaturgy is why so many of us love it – and why so many of us lean on complex metaphors of navigation and midwifery to describe the work. It is also why, despite more theater practitioners incorporating dramaturgy into their work ethic, it is vital to have a dramaturg as an identifiable member of any collaborative, theatrical endeavor. I ended up hiring the interviewee, and now she gets to observe as ten different dramaturgs work on new plays, musicals, and puppet theater. From having never witnessed the concept in action, to now observing ten different embodiments of that concept, my intern will, I hope, leave with an expanded understanding of what it means to be a dramaturg. (And perhaps find the idea of being a dramaturg both more tenable and more tangible.)

Yes, all theater practitioners can, and should, practice dramaturgy, but without a dramaturg in the room, the dramaturgy is limited by being filtered through a different set of priorities and responsibilities. But with a dramaturg, dramaturgy has breath, and life, and agency.

Having collaborated with Theresa Lang for several years now, I have witnessed firsthand her commitment to fostering lively and deep dramaturgy in all areas of the theater. For any students or practitioners interested in embodying both the title and concept of "dramaturg," this book will prove an invaluable resource.

Anne G. Morgan
Literary Manager and Dramaturg
Eugene O'Neill Theater Center

ACKNOWLEDGMENTS

Thank you to the artists, teachers, and students I have worked with who showed me what it means to make collaborative art and to those who shared stories, ideas, and time. I am especially indebted to the dramaturgs I met through the Kennedy Center New Play Dramaturgy Intensive and the Kennedy Center American College Theater Festival. These artists helped me find the language for these ideas. Particular thanks to Mark Bly, Anne Morgan, Tyler Smith, Talya Kingston, Maren Robinson, Dan Burson, Alexis Jade Links, Rachel Hutt, Margot Manburg, and Jessie Baxter. Thank you to my students for helping me work through ways of talking about this approach and to Stacey Walker at Taylor & Francis who believed that approach could make a book. Finally, thank you to my family and friends for the encouragement and support, especially Elisabeth Lang who read every draft. Last but not least, thank you Don and Jackson, for all of it.

Part I

MINDSET

1

FROM NOUN TO VERB

Something happens when you change a noun to a verb. *To kiss* is so much more interesting than *a kiss*. We may enjoy *a run* but we can love *to run*. We can dive, leap, taste, and storm more fully and feel the action as a verb rather than just a noun. It is a linguistic hop, and a conceptual leap – to go from being to doing. Being can be interesting and informative and even all-encompassing, but doing is active and engaged and in the moment. There are numerous words in English that can act as noun or verb, and the essential meaning may change or not, depending on the term. Even when the words mean the same they can have a different connotation; for instance, upstage as a location as opposed to as an action.

In the richness of our language, a whole other term is required when discussing the person who does the action, another word that connotes the doing of the thing. One is not a teach, she is a teacher; not a write but a writer, and a firefighter is one who fights fires. While there is the implied active verb in the name, the role is designated as well. A manager manages, a director directs, and a designer designs.

The exception to the naming practice is the dramaturg. While the discipline is dramaturgy, both the role and the act are called dramaturg. Here is a term that shares the same word between what is done and who does it, and therefore offers an exciting opportunity to make a linguistic connection that reveals the role is the act. This allows us to better understand both role and action. When we shift from noun to verb and see the role as inextricably linked to the action, it becomes clear that dramaturg is something one does; it is simultaneously a process, practice, the person, and the outcome. Its very title requires an acknowledgment of this active nature.

The purpose of this book is to introduce a new way to consider dramaturgy and to offer a critical introduction to both its point of view and its practice. The book explores the mindset that guides the work of the dramaturg and recognizes the important role of the dramaturg in the theatre. This study considers the change in perspective from noun to verb; from something one is to something one does, in order to better understand the nature of dramaturgy and the contribution of the dramaturg to a project. When we move from noun to verb, from being to doing, we are able to conceive dramaturgy as a mindset rather than a function. Dramaturgy is a way of seeing and communicating, a way of engaging with material and audiences, and ultimately a way of looking at the world.

The American theatre has greatly expanded its inclusion of dramaturgs so there is less imperative to justify our place at the table than ever before, although it is still in its developing stages around the country. There are now a variety of examples of this expanding presence, and places like the giant of new play development the Eugene O'Neill Theater Center and the dramaturgy-driven work of the Oregon Shakespeare Theater remind us that this is an exciting time to be a dramaturg. There are currently more training programs and more theatres that include a dramaturgical sensibility as part of their artistic mission than ever before. The presence of the dramaturg is more conspicuous and the contribution more widely recognized. Consequently, it is a good time to explore what the dramaturg can be in and out of the theatre and consider how to both develop the outlook and hone the skills.

It is worth noting that while the level of involvement has increased, dramaturgs still often face the particular challenge of an unusual title and an ambiguous position. It is a somewhat awkward Germanic term that defies simple definition, and it describes a role that is so situation-dependent that we often find ourselves relying on metaphor and analogy to answer what initially appears to be a straightforward question: "What do you do?" This is somewhat inevitably followed with: "What is dramaturgy?" Definition is where we tend to start most classes, conversations, and books on the subject. Perhaps the most colorful labeling of this activity is credited to Michael Mark Chemers' work *Ghost Light* in which the first chapter is titled "What the #$%@ Is a Dramaturg?" While there are more academic programs offering training and degrees in dramaturgy and more professional theatres relying on the contributions of the credited dramaturg, the field still spends many beginnings in definition.

To begin the defining, one of the reasons for the shift from noun to verb is that the noun of dramaturg too often can be reduced to a list of tasks. Sometimes the role may be understood merely as the collection of those tasks and the genuine contribution that a dramaturg makes to a production is ignored. A simplified definition will explain dramaturg through the tangible work product, the quantifiable activities that she does on a production. Consequently, what is dramaturgy is answered as the list of duties that are done by the person designated dramaturg; which could include casebooks, talkbacks, and study guides. There is some value to a definition that allows for concrete aspects, yet the task-based approach is ultimately wanting. Not only does it restrict the scope of understanding the role of dramaturg, it can also ultimately limit the role itself. When the role is defined by the tasks it can easily become relegated to the fulfillment of those tasks and nothing else. Consequently, a narrow, task-based interpretation of the role of a dramaturg in production may allow room for the completion of those set tasks but may actually prevent the dramaturgical presence throughout the production.

However, when we look at the dramaturg with a broader lens, using a more holistic approach, the tasks are merely parts of a larger picture of a way of thinking and doing. This aspect may be called the dramaturgical perspective, approach, mindset, and so on, and what these share is the notion that dramaturgy is a way of being, almost ontological, not merely the completion of the acts.

Even when the conversation goes to the more inclusive artistic role in the production and the definition attempts to go further than the punch list, it is not a question that is easily answered and the answer often relies on analogy or metaphor. There are some poetic and evocative metaphors that dramaturgs use, including images of navigation and cartography. These images can be useful and the analogies offer an interesting context, but as an analogy it is merely a stand-in as meaning. While useful, it is still limited and so different explanations are constantly being formed and modified in attempts to get closer to the referent point, closer to something particular and specific, closer to a mindset.

These definitions, then, deal more with this mindset, or perspective, rather than the collection of tasks. Frequently the dramaturg defines her own work within this frame, and the website of the Literary Managers and Dramaturgs of the Americas (LMDA) has an entire section dedicated to members' answers to the prompt, what is dramaturgy? For the most part, these contributions and those of other dramaturgs talking about their own work offer insight into the kind of work the dramaturgs see for themselves. Some talk about themselves as a facilitator, questioner, explorer, translator, or catalyst. Others describe their ability to provide context, offer insight, and help navigate the world of the play. Mark Bly, the godfather of American dramaturgy, summons Billy Collins' poem "Introduction to Poetry" in his essay "Pressing an Ear Against a Hive or New Play Explorations in the Twenty-First Century" where the ultimate goal of the dramaturg is to approach a play as if it were a new world. It is important to note that it is the mindset of the dramaturg that drives the interpretation and shapes how he operates in a production.

The need to define through description is consistent when dramaturgs discuss their work. Since neither the word nor the role lends itself to concrete and tangible definition, so as dramaturgs we try to offer a context of our general approach to the work, the kinds of conversations and questions and revelations we facilitate. In essence we act like dramaturgs in how we answer the question.

So what is the definition? The ability to define, to offer context, is among the most important traits of the dramaturg. Consequently, some of the best training for the development of a dramaturg lies within its existential nature – inherent in the role is the need to define it. The incessant demand to define this role is where we start, and it is this process that offers some of the best practice for our function. The experience of creating the context of the role, of constructing dimension for a term and an idea that is elusive to the questioner, is itself a way to practice dramaturgy. The definition, then, ends up being both verb and noun, the doer and the outcome.

The first thing to do, then, is to set the parameters of the question. "What is dramaturgy?" necessarily encompasses more than the list of tasks, though those also warrant consideration. Yet the starting point is the viewpoint, the approach, and the *étude* of the dramaturg. What does she bring to the production? How is her place in the room defined? How are his questions framed? What is the unique point of view that the dramaturg can offer? In short, what is the dramaturgical mindset, and more importantly, how does one develop it?

The path to the mindset of the dramaturg is through that process of definition, starting with changing the parameters of the word defined. Rather than define the noun dramaturgy we define the verb to dramaturg. It is a change that refers to the active process the dramaturg undertakes and enables a shift in perspective to open up the possibilities of what dramaturgy can do and how it can be understood. When a person is able to explain the *doing of dramaturgy*, the tangible products of the role can be a useful illustration of the kinds of output a production dramaturg may provide in the course of a production, an example of her work. However, these tasks alone cannot encompass the verb to dramaturg and consequently will not allow for the definition to end with them. The role is elusive and requires context, and useful context can be found with the verb to dramaturg. The verb allows the discussion to be about what we do, not as the list of tasks but as the active perspective on the material, as the way of looking and engaging that is responsive and challenges our audience each step of the way. We call ourselves dramaturgs and study the practice of dramaturgy, and what we do as artists is dramaturg.

Ultimately, the definition is to dramaturg: to curate an experience for an audience.

It is a simple definition that is broad in scope and in its breadth it seems that one can dramaturg virtually anything. This is a useful starting point in understanding the dramaturgical mindset as it is one that relies upon its flexibility and creativity. The process by which the dramaturg curates the experience and the specificity with which the audience is addressed are the benchmarks of its efficacy, but since the process is established by its definition, that process can be applied to any activity.

The straightforward definition still can use some expansion, starting with the choice of the word curate. The selection and organization that is part of "to curate" is an important connection to dramaturgy. The sifting and sorting through material, as well as the persistent editing and reconfiguring of content, is a part of the daily work of the dramaturg, and so connects to the connotations of the notion to curate. There is some reticence to use the term curate in part because of the extensive use and popularity of the word in recent years. It is historically connected to museum curators yet the contemporary use has grown to include almost any kind of gathering or assembling. However, the composition implied in the traditional and contemporary use of the word curate is part of the value it provides in defining dramaturg as verb. It is not merely the collecting of content that curate implies, but its informed selection, purposeful editing, and most important, its designed presentation. While there is an (arguably) over-use of curator as title for a variety of jobs, DJs, furniture stores, and all over ETSY and craft fairs, the word offers an effective point of contact with dramaturgy.

To curate an experience, any experience, relies on the clarity of what characterizes that experience. If one is to dramaturg a production, there is a large-scale action that is taking place, yet within that there are many smaller pieces, more fixed experiences to curate. These may include the experience of the language of the script, the music of the era, or the politics of the community. To perform the overall process well, each piece needs to be dramaturged, and to do that, each experience needs to be framed. The definition, then, includes the experience itself and the parameters of that experience. How does one frame it into a particular and comprehensive whole? What is it that needs curating?

Since one dramaturgs by curating an experience for an audience, the particularity of the audience is another important element for the dramaturg that will be explored. It is a defining point for dramaturg as verb and drives the shape of the project and absolutely determines the manner in which it is delivered. The content is not only selected and organized; it is delivered in a specific way based on the recipient. Who is being spoken to decides the language spoken, and the presentation of material is defined by the recipient of the material. The audience can be any or all members of a production team, the back office, publicity, or any part of the theatrical audience and each project that is dramaturged has a known audience that will determine how the information is shared – what language is spoken.

The move to looking at dramaturg as verb rather than noun opens up the possibility of an active integrated activity that is dramaturgy. It is a way to shape a perspective, a way of seeing that supports flexible thinking and helps one become a more effective member of the creative team.

The definition of dramaturg as verb corresponds with a three-step method to doing it. Each of the three steps is as important as the others and each needs to be executed fully for effective dramaturgy. The method will be developed more fully in a later chapter; however, the following are the three steps.

- First, the dramaturg sets the parameters of the project.
- Second, the dramaturg compiles the information needed for that project.
- Third, the dramaturg constructs the most effective mode of presentation for that information.

This straightforward process will help to keep the dramaturg on track and stay effective. It is a process that offers the tools to keep the dramaturgy thoroughly linked to the project. The dramaturg both guides and responds to the audience experience through the development process.

First, you set the parameters of the project, and define your role at the beginning and throughout the process. The process to dramaturg necessarily starts with definition and the best way to establish effective dramaturgy is to define the role as clearly as possible. This is a role that is completely case-dependent; it is up to the particular needs of the project to determine how its dramaturgy will be defined. This first step requires clarity of purpose more than anything. We ask the question: "What is this for?" in order to answer fully the question: "What is this?" Self-reflection is key to this step. The specific circumstances of the project and thus the particular circumstances to dramaturg are formed through the clear understanding of the end goal; what is the need being met by this dramaturgy? Once that is understood, the particular ways the role will serve the project can then be articulated and then communicated to others.

The next step is the one that most closely resembles the series of tasks that so often stand in for a workable definition of dramaturgy. The second step is the gathering and editing of content. Once the project has been defined, we begin to ask and answer questions through the various avenues available. You begin to engage with others around you – director, actors, designers or whoever the project collaborators may be. This step in the process is what many of the analogies and elevator speeches are referring to. It is the research part of dramaturgy.

It is the chance to find context, historical and political circumstances, meaning, and convention. It is the opportunity to push out past the limitations of the script into the world of the both the play and the production. It is the step on which we spend a lot of our time and energy. An important thing to remember in this step is that it is predicated on the first step. The project's definition is what shapes the content. Dramaturg as verb relies on focused and purpose-driven research. The content sought is the particular pieces that support the project as defined.

The final step of the process is to determine and construct the way to share our content with the intended audience. Is it a text-based or visual medium? Is it a physical artifact or an electronic file? What shape does it take and what does it look like? These are all questions we ask in order to decide upon the best way to share what we have found. Once again the answer is determined by the parameters of the project and the intended audience. The same information for an actor and an audience is going to have different needs and thus different mode of presentation. The best content is not effective if the delivery of that content is not useful.

We expand the definition beyond the metaphor or the task. To dramaturg is to curate an experience for an audience. We do that by identifying the project, finding the content, and presenting it to our audience.

There are plenty of opportunities to look at the tasks typically associated with the dramaturg and define the role based on those tasks. There is the trap of: "The dramaturg is the one who does research on the world of the play and creates the lobby display." Or, to use an interesting and evocative metaphor to try to encapsulate what she does in the production: "The dramaturg is the cartographer of the production, helping to chart the path the play will forge." These can be useful shortcuts in conversation and explanation but do offer merely an abbreviated version at best of what dramaturgy is and what the dramaturg does, and underplay the added depth that an effective dramaturg brings to a production and an audience's experience.

It seems that the most useful entry point into practicing effective dramaturgy is to understand that it is a mindset and a creative role that understands and respects the creative responsibilities of the other artists. While the skills brought to the production through research and

display are undoubtedly necessary, dramaturgy is also the way of looking at the world and approaching a given situation. The most effective
way to be useful in the room is when one is prepared to dramaturg.

Perhaps the most significant opportunity of dramaturg as a term is
that those who do it can define it. It is a word that is strange in its pronunciation, sometimes inconsistent in its spelling, and often vague in
its definition. And one that is better understood as a verb.

Essential Dramaturgy: The Mindset and Skillset is geared primarily to
the dramaturgy student and early career professional as a way to shift
the discussion of the role and introduce a methodology for an invested,
holistic approach to the work. It will also likely appeal to collaborators
who are looking for ways to more effectively incorporate dramaturgy
into their process. In addition it is presented to practitioners to continue the conversation about ways to think about dramaturgy.

This book is intended to be a companion to the theoretical and
practical guides on the market. It will explore ways to develop the perspective of an artistic collaborator, and offer some "how tos" toward
that development. Among the works it joins are two of the foundational theoretical guides: *The Production Notebooks* edited by Mark Bly
and *Toward a Dramaturgical Sensibility* by Geoffrey Proehl. The practical
guides include Michael Mark Chemers' *Ghost Light*, which offers a
strong academic and analytical context to the practice of dramaturgy
while *The Process of Dramaturgy: A Handbook* by Scott Irelan, Anne
Fletcher, and Julie Felise Dubiner gives the reader a straightforward
"how to" of the tasks of the dramaturg. Some other useful approaches
to the craft and examples of its execution include *The Art of Active
Dramaturgy* by Leonora Inez Brown and *The Routledge Companion to
Dramaturgy* edited by Magda Romanska.

This book is meant to continue the discussion of dramaturgy, a discussion that has been happening since Lessing's *Hamburg Dramaturgy* and
is currently up for dynamic debate in journals, in blogs, and on online
theatre communities like HowlRound (HowlRound.com). *Ghost
Light* and the Introduction to *The Routledge Companion to Dramaturgy*
both offer good historical contexts of the term and the development
of dramaturgy in the American theatre. This work takes that context
and seeks to shift the way dramaturgy is discussed as a tool to understand more fully what it means to dramaturg. The tone of the text is
also intended to reflect a discussion. The content has been refined in

practice and conversation over the course of time and this book is the translation of that narrative into readable form. Consequently, there are elements that are "how tos" directed to the reader, as well as inclusive conversations about what we do as dramaturgs.

Essential Dramaturgy is organized in two sections.

Part I is an examination of the mindset to dramaturg and it breaks down the various components to develop that perspective. Chapter 2 looks at the way the dramaturg uses questions in relationship to the text, production team, and audience. Chapter 3 considers the dramaturgical approach as a broad-based and encompassing point of reference where one is able to offer a holistic viewpoint. Chapter 4 examines the importance of timing in working on a production. Chapter 5 investigates the idea of "why this play, here, now?" in the dramaturg's work.

Part II analyzes some of the tasks of the dramaturg and explores ways to approach those tasks with the mindset and process of dramaturg as verb. Chapter 6 breaks down the three-step method to dramaturg. Chapter 7 considers how this can be applied to the work done with artistic collaborators through the production cycle. Chapter 8 takes on the tasks that are audience-directed and applies the model of dramaturg as verb. Chapter 9 encounters working on new plays and devised projects. Chapter 10 is a collection of shared stories, using anecdotes and tips for developing as a dramaturg.

The book is a result of more than a decade of development as a dramaturg and reflecting on the meaning of the work and how it enhances theatrical production. Working, teaching, and discussing dramaturgy has provided the opportunity to see how the field is maturing. After many hours spent with student and professional dramaturgs, sharing stories and talking about the nature of the field, it became clear this was an experience that needed to be shared. This work is an attempt to dramaturg that experience.

2

QUESTIONS ASKED AND ANSWERED

"What does this have to do with us?" the dramaturg asks during the production meeting after the sound designer has talked about some of the potential musical selections. The question has become something of a habit for the meetings now and causes the production staff to take a pause and then discuss the options and other alternatives. The dramaturg asks the same thing at rehearsal at least once a week and the question is a touchstone of the collaborative process. The play is about teenagers; however, it is very far removed from the realities of the college audience, and finding points of connection has become a primary goal of the production team, consistently reinforced in production choices, prompted by the dramaturg asking, "What does this have to do with us?"

The mindset to dramaturg is demonstrated through the question. Questions are essential to the dramaturgical process, and sometimes it is as if the dramaturg's currency is questions. While the dramaturg's work is mostly associated with the context he provides, it is the questions he asks even more than those he answers that develop the point of view to dramaturg. As dramaturgs we ask questions to drive our own research, we ask questions to spark conversation, and we ask questions to inspire and challenge our audience, whoever that may be. The example above shows the dramaturg using a question to keep the production on point and provide a conceptual rallying cry.

Questions are a way to engage. They provide an entry point into a subject and a frame of reference for a conversation. The ability to parse, unravel, and direct the question – either one that we are asking or one that we are answering – is elemental to the dramaturgical mindset. Information is mined and shared through questions, and the overall conceptual frame of the production and the nature of the dramaturgy are supported by an active exchange of questions and answers. For the dramaturg, the ability to unpack a question is largely predicated on the ability to think flexibly and see what/when/why the question arises.

The dramaturg has two categories of questions that she deals with in an artistic collaboration.

- Questions to answer.
- Questions to ask.

A visible part of the dramaturg's role in the production, and one more easily defined as part of her responsibilities, is to gather the contextual information for the company – the dramaturg as the provider of the context. A lot of time is spent finding and fielding questions that need to be answered. What is the historical significance of this artifact? What is the thematic meaning of that reference? The other equally important if not as visible category of question is that which needs to be asked. It is vital to the mindset to dramaturg, the questions she asks help to shape our understanding of and contribution to the project. How is this going to affect the audience? What is the implication of that choice? She asks questions that prompt an answer or elicit information. In addition, she asks questions not meant to be answered, but to take the listener through a creative exploration.

There is a difference between the questions to ask and those to answer and this difference may be the most important distinction for the mindset to dramaturg. Questions are a way to negotiate the various relationships – with the text, production team, and audience – and they have an important function in the creative process. There is concrete data that needs to be shared and understood in order to strengthen the context of a production. There are also philosophical musings that can shape the experience of the production. There are questions that resist direct response that can help shape the movement of the piece. The navigation through these various kinds of questions is integral to how to dramaturg, and knowing when to ask and when to answer is a skill that continues to develop.

The purpose of the question determines whether it is something that needs to be asked or answered, and once that is established the next step is to determine how to proceed. How does the dramaturg ask the question? How does she give the answer? These are equally important and if the question is not asked or answered in an effective manner, the work up to that point is largely in vain. The ability to identify the need and answer the question is only as strong as the dramaturg's delivery, so this aspect is of utmost importance. The key to finding how to ask or answer the question is the audience. The specificity of delivery is as important as the pertinence of the question or accuracy of the answer and that delivery is going to be dependent on who it is for.

The mindset to dramaturg is formed through understanding the need of the audience in order to investigate the question more effectively and direct the transmission of information. For example, the questions we answer require attention to the *who*, as even a simple content question is significantly different when received by different audiences. If we answer a question about the symptoms of tuberculosis, the actor needs information that will let him mimic them, the designer is looking for a way to show the effects of those symptoms on the physical world, a technician may need to know if there is movement that affects the construction, and the audience may need to know stages of the illness to understand how sick the character really is. So how that bit of information – symptoms of tuberculosis – is found and shared will depend on our awareness of the needs of the audience who receives it.

The questions we ask are also based on who the question is aimed at, and require a careful attention to what they are intended to prompt. Once again a simple example demonstrates this with a question meant to generate thought about character – does she love him? This query presented early in the production schedule potentially challenges the director to find a way to create a solid answer through blocking. It can inspire the actor to coordinate the answer to this as part of her objective. The question may activate a design choice that creates a visual connection between the two characters. Presented to the theatrical audience it may inspire them to view the play through the lens of a story about this love.

The overall goal is to develop the mindset to dramaturg in order to become a more effective creative collaborator; part of that comes from understanding that to dramaturg is a mindset itself. It is a way to look at and engage with material that allows for flexible thinking and creative input and output. It is a method of communication and connection as an artistic collaborator. The mindset is characterized by the use of questions. It is a way to analyze a situation and navigate relationships, and it is a process to find the pertinent questions that need to be answered as well as those that need to be asked.

This chapter will look at both categories of questions and consider techniques to approach them. The purpose is to examine some of the ways the mindset can be developed through the relationship to the question, not be a comprehensive guide to dramaturging with questions. The chapter is broken up into sections and starts with a look at the kinds of questions dramaturgs answer, then considers some of the questions the dramaturg asks.

Questions Dramaturgs Answer

The questions the dramaturg answers are typically related to content. The questions are those that are directly asked by a collaborator, the ones the dramaturg assumed would be needed, and the ones he finds himself that will be a useful contribution to the production. The questions come from many different directions, and more importantly, the answers come from a wide variety of sources. This is essential for the dramaturg – content is everywhere and it is the dramaturg's own creativity and flexible thinking that will mine the best sources for the answers he seeks.

TIP: If it can be googled it does not need a dramaturg.

The collection of the answers becomes the material output for the production team, particularly the casebook. The casebook is the collection of information about the playwright, play and world of the production compiled as reference material for the production team, and will be discussed in more depth in a later chapter. A large portion of this information is the answers to the questions that arise from script and company. The contextual data, particular references, and conceptual ideas that characterize the production are generally curated for the company from the answers to a whole series of questions the dramaturg uncovered and was directly asked.

From the Text

The dramaturg starts with the text, unless there is not a text, in which case she starts with the source material or the ensemble. However, for the purposes of this study, the primary examples to illustrate the ideas will be production and new play dramaturgy and these generally start with the text. Many of the questions the dramaturg answers are from the text, and these are the questions that help shape her understanding as well as the input she gives and output she provides her collaborators.

The first relationship the dramaturg establishes is with the script, and that relationship is formed in the first read. A first read is the chance to hear the story, to see how the workings of the play reveal character and action. It is the opportunity to meet the play on its own terms and see what it has to say. The first read is when we experience the tension joining with the celebration of Agamemnon's return, heralded by the watchman at the opening of Aeschylus's *Agamemnon*. It is when we are introduced to the appearance of a playful banter from Lincoln and Booth in *Topdog/Underdog* by Suzan-Lori Parks. The first read is when we experience the play in text form, as the audience will see it, as new and self-revealing.

The mindset to dramaturg is evident in the reading of the text and is developed by approaching the work on its own terms. The dramaturg reads the play the playwright wrote and strives to continue to interact with it on those terms. It is a reading that seeks to see without bias and expectation and the reader meets the text in an open and responsive frame of mind. The dramaturg allows the play to reveal the rules of the world it creates. He focuses on the terms offered by the playwright and so the questions he notes are generally tools to better understand those terms. The questions are not the details of a specialized perspective; they are ones that expand the understanding of the play by examining its parameters. There is no attempt to create a "conceptual" dramaturg, or dramaturg as auteur – these may work for directing, but are not conducive to a mindset to dramaturg. Instead, as dramaturgs we immerse ourselves in the world created by the playwright to better understand how to tease it out and contribute to the creation of a dynamic and whole production. Which means experiencing the play as it is, as constructed by playwright.

We encounter the play as a complete whole, as a story unfolding. Looking at the play as a whole is one of the essential elements of the mindset to dramaturg. Even as we take it apart to analyze the pieces, there is a sense of the work in its entirety that needs to be sustained. Whatever that text offers in terms of form or motif, there is the glimpse of the world of the play, the world that can be mined in order to offer the most useful guideposts for the production to bring it to an audience. This is done primarily through the questions to answer. There are a variety of approaches to script analysis that offer a whole spectrum of literary, artistic, intellectual, and visceral explorations of the work. These methods are tools to find our way into the structure and meaning of the text and are accomplished through a careful question and answer phase between dramaturg and script.

> TIP: Let the script reveal itself. The first time through allow yourself to be immersed in story and character.

Initial questions include genre, style, and theme. What kind of information about the world of the play is necessary to explore the structure and composition of the story? The first questions of the text are those, unraveling the nuance of structure, character, idea, and mood. Looking at the play as a whole, how are the pieces arranged in its composition and how can you tease them out in a way that will offer greater support to the play as a text for the production? The fundamental question for the text in the initial read(s) is: What are the rules of the play?

The questions that reveal the rules of the play also touch on the world of the play and how it is constructed. These are the questions of story, plot, and action and they ask how the story is told structurally and further explore the conditions of the play. The dramaturg answers questions that uncover the basic ingredients of the piece: story, time, character, language, image, theme, and form.

The next questions go another layer into the text. This level of inquiry relates to the style of the play and how story, character, and language function. These questions help to continue to familiarize oneself with the play and derive from a flexible, holistic read of the piece, one that is taking the script as written with as few predisposed ideas as possible. The questions form a practical analysis that demonstrates the manner in which the narrative is constructed. For the most part, the analysis is limited in the first read, which is primarily for story and general impressions. More detailed script analysis typically takes place in subsequent reads, though before conversations with the director or other members of the production team if possible.

After the introduction to the story and the world the playwright created, script analysis gives the tools to start the practical analysis of the text. This book does not go into a methodology for that kind of work with the text; that is a subject that has already been well covered in other works. One of the best manuals for script-reading is David Ball's *Backwards and Forwards*. It is a book that remains an industry standard more than thirty years after its publication and is an incredibly effective guide to how plays work. Another useful guide is the chapter on script analysis in Michael Mark Chemers's *Ghost Light*. Both of these works provide technical instruction on how to examine the text, and the strength of both is that they are committed to the script as dramatic text for performance, so it is a theatrical, not a literary, analysis.

Whatever methodology the dramaturg uses, script analysis offers the tools to investigate the form and content of the play. It explores given circumstances (who, what, where, when, why) to piece together the story structure. In addition the dramaturg seeks the keys to determine theme and metaphor in the piece, as well as identify the spine and recognize patterns. The questions for the play encompass a practical understanding of its construction. Some of those questions include:

- What is the play about?
- Whose play is it?
- What are the rules of this world?
- How do time and space operate in this story and this world?

Once the dramaturg has the fundamental structure of story, she looks for ways to discuss the organizing principle of the play as well as the theoretical framework. The purpose of this series of questions is to answer them for herself, to discern a vocabulary with which to discuss the play. We ask questions to reveal structure, style, energy, music and meaning. These offer insight into the practical considerations of putting it on its feet by delving into time and place and character from a structural sense.

It is not only the structural elements that are answerable questions from the text. Additionally useful in developing the mindset are those that encompass the creation of the play. These questions are vital to understanding the context of the work and are the foundation for the kind of context the dramaturg brings to the company. Among these questions:

- In what ways does it reflect the time and place in which it was created?
- How do the circumstances of its creation influence form or content?
- What about the social or theatrical conventions are displayed in the text?
- What political, historical, or theoretical happening helps shape the play?

These questions all have answers that give context for the script and aid the collaboration by adding to the conversations about the play. The world of the creation of the play is often as informative and integral to understanding meaning as the world of the play. At the same time this context also reveals the value of exploring the same circumstances around the creation of the production.

It is important to uncover the questions from the text as part of seeing the overall picture of the play and also to start the connection between the world of the play and the world of the production. It is that intersection that is ultimately going to be the most significant element and so the dramaturg's input is tailored to that connection, even as she is experiencing the script on its own terms. To dramaturg is to bring those things together, to understand and unpack the script in such a way as to reveal the markers for the production. It is a way to illuminate the ideas the text implies in order to better assist the rest of the production team in exploring them on stage.

Two of the things that affect the mindset to dramaturg are very practical issues.

- What questions to answer?
- How does one find them?

These practical issues connect directly back to reading the text without a lens that narrows the scope. Look at the play as a composite and immerse yourself in the whole of the piece. Do not approach the work looking for the clues that a designer needs to help her create the visual landscape. Do not seek traits or cues of language and context to flesh out a particular characterization as an actor. Do not look for the intimations of composition or pacing that may inform the work of the director. Instead the dramaturg reads the play looking for the clues specific to this play, using an approach that suits her style and is conducive to the particularities of the specific text. The mindset to dramaturg is a way to have an open and flexible relationship to what the playwright offers us in a manner that allows for a view of the whole. The questions, then, rely on the composition of the whole. Consequently, the questions to answer are any point of clarification or illustration that will make the whole more cohesive and comprehensible to an audience.

So how to find them? Once again, flexible thinking is paramount. No two plays are the same and while an individual tends to develop a way of working, that process needs to include room to treat each new text based on the needs of that text. The questions are found in the initial response to the work. They come from the guideposts that the playwright provides to tell the story and construct the world of the play. They come from the attention to the cues of how time and space are treated in the world of the play. They arise from the understanding of character interaction and relationship as a narrative mode. The questions from the text are the spaces in between the mosaic pieces of the play's construction. When reading with a dramaturgical eye, we have the privilege to look at both, the pieces of the composition and the spaces in between them. One of the ways we find the mindset to dramaturg is in the practice of teasing the questions from the spaces in between and helping to bring those to the story of the production.

Some of the given circumstances questions to answer from the text as preliminary orientation to the story:

- Who are these people? How are they revealed?
- Where are we? What are the spatial and locational realities?
- What is the action? What changes? What is the conflict?
- When does this take place? How does time play out and what time, date, year do we move through?
- Why is this story told? What makes this day different than others?
- What is the play about? Not in terms of plot or even action, but what Aristotle called thought. What is the meaning?

The questions are situated in the structure of the play. The dramaturg uses the tools of script analysis and an exploration of the rules of the play and the rules of the world in which it has been created in order to uncover those questions. The given circumstances offer the building blocks of content and show her where the questions of story and plot may be examined. In addition, the theatrical conventions give insight into how the text is assembled and provide necessary information about form.

Questions are in the script, and an understanding of and attention to form and content meets the intuitive and imaginative relationship to the text in a way that allows us to mine the questions we need to answer. The mindset to dramaturg relies on questions, and that starts from our first exposure to the script. The above questions are content clarification, for the most part, and it is what follows that reveals more about the outlook to dramaturg since it relies more heavily on the *how* than on the *why*. How is this story structured, how is that character revealed, how do we learn the rules of this world are more useful approaches to dramaturging a text than asking why those choices were made. There are times in which the question why is effective; however, for our relationship to the text, how seems to be a stronger tool.

The Production Team

The dramaturg should be prepared to be a useful resource for the production team from early in the production cycle. A measure of effectiveness is seen in the kinds of questions the production team asks. Sometimes those questions will be factual such as, "What kind of writing materials would have been used for a letter in the seventeenth century?" Other times it might be conceptual, "Does the movement sequence feel as if it comes out of nowhere in the second act?" Whatever kinds of questions come from the production team, the dramaturg offers a responsive perspective, and typically it will take the form of an answer. An open and responsive relationship will generally make for a better artistic collaboration. The most important aspect of this question and answer relationship is to understand what is being asked.

A director's questions for the dramaturg can cover a wide range of topics. It is vital that the dramaturg stay connected to the motion of the production in order to have clear access to the context of the question. Sometimes a seemingly small detail-based question can reveal a wide array of information and content that can inform the next phase of the production. A too narrow scope, or being out of touch with the development of the process, may become a missed opportunity to bring that scope into the room and ultimately to the audience. For example, a question about the history of a musical genre can reveal a significant class division based on who listened to what at a certain time and can clarify a tension and significantly alter the way that relationships are played out on stage. It can do that if the answer comes in an effective way and the dramaturg understands the implication. At other times the director's questions may be explicit requests to watch for something happening on stage – and the dramaturg's answers must address the request but also reflect an understanding of the larger production.

A question asked that seems simple does not need to be made complex, but it does need to be parsed to discover the larger structure it is supporting. A question about military protocol can translate into a more crisp and precise blocking pattern for an entire play. The way to assess a question, the way to translate what is being asked, is a key aspect to the mindset to dramaturg.

> TIP: *The question the dramaturg does not answer is a request for an opinion of an artistic choice.*

The dramaturg offers insight into the world of the production by answering questions and giving input about the world of the play. He does this by maintaining a holistic view of both, and practicing useful response to what is given on its own terms. The key word here is useful. The answers have clear intent and are crafted to be directly beneficial to the production. Consequently, even the traditional dramaturgical research provided to the company – like the casebook – is more than a compilation of data. How to approach these tasks is another way to develop the mindset to dramaturg. The particulars of creating the casebook are addressed in a later chapter, although it is worth mentioning that the casebook provides the source of connection between the questions from the text and those from the company. The questions will inform the dramaturg of the needs and perspective of the company as much as the answers will inform the company about the context of the work. Attention to the relationships and processes of the company will reveal the ongoing needs. Merely offering the definition of a word to an actor can be valuable, but that does not necessarily answer the question being asked. The nuance and significance of a particular word being used, for example a term that indicates a class-based insult in the context of the play, adds depth to a relationship. The kinds of questions the actors, designers, management, and technicians have are need-based questions – even the ones they have not asked yet. Understanding the need allows the dramaturg to respond to it.

The questions from the company come from a specific need for input or content that can help further the artistic process. An actor needs a social context in order to better understand his role in a complex relationship dynamic, a designer is looking for how something would have been used in order to determine a wear pattern to show age, a technician needs to understand the logistics of a weapon's use in order to rig the necessary equipment. The question asked, or not yet asked, will have the specific purpose driving it, so to successfully dramaturg is to mine that purpose as well. The questions from the company are typically not simple, straightforward answers that could be found with a quick generalized search. That is a search that will tell us how to pronounce a word but not why the choice of that word is culturally significant. When a dramaturg effectively unpacks the question, it allows him to discover the *why* at issue and so he can answer the question asked, and direct the answer to the need behind the question.

Earlier in the chapter the symptoms of tuberculosis were used as an example of a research question for an actor or designer to know how to play or indicate the affliction. However, the question about the symptoms of an illness can go beyond the practical need to perform the symptoms. What the research and conversation reveals about the cause, additional complications, and the social attitudes towards that illness can provide a much deeper resonance in the design and the playing of that element. If a character goes on a journey, that is an important contextual element. When the distance and terrain of a journey are understood, that can drastically change the design choices as well as the physicality for a character. There is nothing in the dramaturg's answers that is unrelated to the world of the play that the production team is bringing to the stage.

The examples and kinds of questions noted from the director and the company are primarily the content-based "research" work, the task that is so often identified as the work of the dramaturg. The questions the dramaturg fields are not limited to these kinds of practical and particular needs, but they offer a good illustration of the way to approach a question that utilizes and develops the mindset to dramaturg. Once there is an outlook based on flexible and responsive thinking, the dramaturg can apply the process to the variety of inquiries that come her way from the various sources.

The Audience

Another important source of questions to answer is the theatrical audience. This group is one on whom the dramaturg can have direct influence and there is a significant opportunity for communication. This can be direct contact, with questions answered through marketing and audience outreach materials. In addition, it can be an indirect process, where the dramaturg is answering the perceived questions in feedback to the production team when acting as surrogate for the eventual audience in the rehearsal room. The kind of question the audience might have about the relevance of a ritual or the clarity of a social practice is the kind of thing she brings up in rehearsal to enable the production to answer the question before it might be asked. In the same way the dramaturg anticipates the kinds of things from the text that will raise questions, she watches for things in the production that will be questions to answer for the audience. In all instances, the questions and answers need to be framed in a way that is most effective for the production.

TIP: It is OK to not know the answer.

The dramaturg has the end point of an audience viewing the production in mind throughout the process and one of her responsibilities is to anticipate the questions that need to be answered for that audience and identify the best way to do so. There are a series of avenues available, in the production itself, as mentioned, as well as through the outreach material. The in-production questions and discussion are often about the structure of the narrative and its telling. To build these tools effectively these are the questions of clarification the dramaturg asks the director or other members of the production team throughout the process. The dramaturg serves as an early proxy for the audience to see what is clear and what creates a further question from seeing the production. These questions of clarity also shape the content or context answers to deliver in pre- and post-show talkbacks, lobby displays, or program notes, all of which are examined in more detail in a later chapter. These outreach materials are a way to speak directly to the audience and provide a narrative of the production. Being present in the rehearsal room gives access to the work being done as well as access to what is intended, so the dramaturg has a unique perspective on the work in progress. Ultimately the dramaturg watches to see how the story is shaped, how the production is working from a narrative standpoint, as well as how it conveys what is intended by the director.

The questions to answer, from the text, for the production team, and for the audience all have something in common; they are all tools to clarify the story. The clues in the text are revealed to help actors, director, and designers embody them more effectively and the questions answered for the audience all point to a more complete theatrical experience. The dramaturg answers questions that need to be answered, those he is asked and those he anticipates.

Questions Dramaturgs Ask

Dramaturgs ask questions. It is fundamentally what we do as dramaturgs. We ask questions to mine information and we frequently give feedback in the form of a question – it is a way to give a note that inspires our collaborator to consider new ideas rather than offering a proscriptive solution. Purposely we sometimes ask questions that cannot be answered, but instead are intended to spark a conversation, or a response. We ask questions to make sure that everyone is working toward the same end goal. In addition, asking questions is a way to strengthen the connections between subjects – collaborators as well as director to text, designer to audience. Dramaturgs ask questions as a fundamental tool to dramaturg.

Of the Text

There are a series of questions that the dramaturg answers from text, using whatever methods of script analysis and content gathering is applicable. In addition, she asks questions of the text and this process is instrumental in developing the mindset. The way to approach the cues and questions of the text shapes the process into a decidedly dramaturgical read which is important to the relationship with the text. While actors, directors, designers and technicians read with a particular viewpoint, to read as a dramaturg means to look at the text holistically. It is not the sum of the parts of production cues, narrative structure, and character traits, it is a larger whole of the composition of the story told by the playwright, arranged as a text for performance. The dramaturg asks questions that reveal the nature of the rules of the play as depicted by the playwright. Similarly, she asks questions about the production cues. The fact that it is a text for performance is an important element for the dramaturg, and she stays connected to the notion that reading the script is a placeholder for the play embodied in performance. It is not an exercise in literary analysis, but recognizing the text as a blueprint for performance. Consequently, the questions she asks are of a written text, but for a dynamic performance.

Some questions the dramaturg may ask of the text:

- How do time and place operate? How do they affect the characters?
- What are the key images or metaphors of the piece?
- How are tone and style indicated?
- Where and how do we learn about characters?
- What are the keys to story, character, and idea and how are they situated in the play?
- What is the movement, and when does it change?

The questions we ask of the text are not as concrete as the given circumstances and are not as directly answered. They are ways to connect more profoundly to the choices the playwright made, to see the terms on which the script is constructed and immerse oneself more completely into the text for performance.

Of the Director

The mindset to dramaturg is established through creating the relationship to the material and the audience that allows for the kind of responsiveness that will be useful on a production. This is particularly evident in the role of questions of the director. The effectiveness with which we use the question is a main source of determining the effectiveness of the dramaturgy.

There are some similarities in the way directors and dramaturgs approach text and some overlap of point of view in rehearsal. However, the roles are distinct and it is worth taking a moment to separate their function. Effective collaboration is more likely when all parties are clear on what and how the disparate roles function and the conflicts that arise often do so because there is not agreement on how the positions complement each other. The director guides the production to the performance. She provides the overall vision of the show and works with the rest of the production team to combine artistic elements to bring that vision to an audience. She is looking with the view of how to make it work, what needs to happen in terms of aesthetics, blocking, and composition in order to tell the story of the play. The dramaturg is also looking with the idea of presenting the story for the audience, but his responsibility is not to guide the production, rather it is to help ensure the company has the necessary tools to make the journey.

A fundamental tool the dramaturg offers the director is the questions he asks. These questions include two types, those that expect an answer and those that do not. They should be incisive and provocative and much of the working relationship is likely going to depend on the effective use of questions. As discussed in the previous chapter, it is a role that depends on the ability to develop and expand creative relationships, and every relationship and thus every process is going to be different. In fact, while there is a manner of working that an artist develops over time, the relationship with directors is largely determined by personality, style, and collaborative process. With that understanding of difference, and taking into consideration that who the director is will shape how to frame the question, here are a couple of examples of the kinds of questions a dramaturg may ask the director.

What Are You Reading?

The director does her research on the play and the overlap of sources and content can be useful in conversations about the production. Also, when the dramaturg knows what kinds of additional material outside the script are being used as influences in the production it increases his understanding of and connection to the whole production. Consequently, one of the questions that request an answer to ask the director is what she is looking at, listening to, and reading.

What Do You See in the Play?

This is another question to ask and will hopefully spark an extended conversation. This kind of open-ended question covers a lot of possibilities and can lead to discussion on form or content. Larger thematic elements, symbols or metaphor, relationships or elements of story can all be elicited by this question and it will give the dramaturg a sense of where the director sees the work, which is the kind of information that will help to identify early on the preliminary groundwork of the production.

Then throughout the production process we as dramaturgs ask the director additional questions. Early in the production we ask in order to get information about the director's notions for the production and thoughts about the text. Also, these early questions and conversations help generate ideas about the kind of input the company will need to better realize this vision. During the rehearsal process we ask the questions that help reinforce that her goals for the production are being served. We ask if she sees what we see at a certain point in a rehearsal. We ask the questions that help to maintain the connection between the production and the director's vision for that production.

Another fundamental use of the question for the director is feedback. As a general rule, it is more useful to give feedback to the director as questions. An essential characteristic of the mindset to dramaturg is that it is responsive, not proscriptive. It is a way of seeing that relies on both clarity and the ability to respond to what is seen, not what was expected. When we work with a director on a production we are offering creative input to augment her architecture. So rather than declarative commentary or suggestion, we ask questions that clarify, inform, or challenge. The questions we ask are intended to help that architecture expand into a theatrical event for an audience. Since the dramaturg is watching a rehearsal with the thematic and conceptual content in mind, the questions are going to be grounded more in the overall impression of a moment than the specifics of, for instance, the blocking for a single actor. For example, the dramaturg may ask, "Do you see this as the moment that she becomes really isolated from the other characters?" It is the kind of question that alludes to a blocking choice, perhaps, and indicates how the dramaturg perceives the scene as staged. The same kind of responsiveness can be more direct, such as, "He looks to me like he is really threatening to hit him, is that what you are hoping to see?"

Using the form of a question to share feedback is a good way to avoid potential conflict. When dramaturgical response appears to be directing or acting notes, it becomes less effective. While it is sometimes difficult to navigate, the notion is simple – the dramaturg is not there to direct the show. His input does not tell the director the solution to a staging quandary; the dramaturg brings to the rehearsal a perspective that helps to create an environment of collaborative, context-rich playmaking.

The questions the dramaturg asks the director should be insightful and provocative. They should inspire thought and conversation and be the vehicle of creative input and collaboration. The specific needs of the production and style of both director and dramaturg will determine how this process is most effective and it is a good reminder that the subject of the question is a significant source for determining the nature of the question. Who we are speaking with, and what we are trying to accomplish, is a useful guide for what and how we ask the question.

The specifics of working with a playwright will be discussed in a later chapter, but it warrants mention here that the relationship with the writer is similar to the relationship with the director in terms of developing the mindset to dramaturg. When working on a script in any capacity, the close understanding of the intent and the open approach to the methodology of the playwright are extremely useful in effective collaboration as a dramaturg. The dramaturg is there to assist the playwright in crafting the play he wants to write; it is not a co-writing relationship any more than it is a co-directing role in production dramaturgy. The dramaturg has his own role, questions are his currency, and they come from a perspective that has a close, knowledgeable, and invested relationship with the material.

Of the Production Team

The questions for the company are by necessity questions of clarification and response. Dramaturgs use this forum to bring attention to the points of connection between the stage and the audience, and to help maintain the link between the world of the play and the world of the production – however that has been forged. The questions we try to find are those that can help connect the landscape and the movement of the production more completely to the play and the audience. We ask questions based on a holistic approach to the production and a viewpoint that is focused on what is shown rather than what is expected.

The ability to respond to what is given is particularly important when conveying questions the audience might have to the production team. The questions raised are not based on expectations of how something will be carried out, but on how the action unfolds. When sitting proxy for the audience the dramaturg responds to moments that may create pause, that potentially take the audience member into a direction that is unintended. These questions, then, are raised in the rehearsal in order to flag those moments for the director and performers. The question is not based on how an issue can be solved, and once again, often the job is to ask the question, not answer it. However, the specialized position in the rehearsal allows for the dramaturg to be the advance look for a later audience and the first call of the production-based question. The role is not to look for problems or offer solutions, but to be a viewer who is invested in the production, with a voice that can offer creative input – and a useful question.

Does the audience see the ghost in *Hamlet*? While this is an artistic decision that is ultimately the director's, it is the kind of question that connects play and production and has conceptual implications that extend beyond the choice itself. If the audience does not see the ghost of the dead king, do they assume it is in Hamlet's mind, a sign of insanity? If they do, is the image frightening? This is a question that is a lynchpin for a series of production choices and has implications on character and action. The best questions the dramaturg asks the production team have implications on aesthetic and narrative.

In unpacking the question we want to dramaturg, we need to be in close contact with the production team, and also continue to develop our understanding of the roles in production. In the same way that practicing various approaches to script analysis will help uncover the questions from the text, the close attention to the process of actors and directors with whom we work helps to refine the questions we ask those individuals. A function of the dramaturg is to add to the creative stretch and practical need of the production, and understanding how our co-creators work enables the most useful dramaturgy and allows for the most effective collaboration.

Of the Audience

The questions for the audience are inherent in the production, they are the places and ideas that challenge the audience to think, feel, and/ or respond. This is a part of the production that the entire creative team is working toward, and when we dramaturg we are helping to keep those points sharp and direct. In the audience outreach materials like the program note, lobby display or marketing materials, we have a further opportunity to ask the audience questions. These can be about their experience or provocative questions to spark additional thought and conversation. While outreach materials should not be explaining the production, they can be additional points of reference for connecting the audience to the play, inside and outside the theatre.

The fundamental questions for the audience come from the production, and the dramaturg can add to those through direct-contact materials and provoke the audience to think about the next question. When there is a play that deals with an important and controversial subject, sometimes the most important question for the audience is, "What are you going to do about it?"

Rules for Questions: Asked and Answered

Here are some things to think about when looking at the questions to answer and to ask as a dramaturg. It is merely a sample of the kinds of rules we establish in our collaborations, and can be useful to think about how to apply the work.

The Magic Word Is Efficacy

The work must be useful. All content and communication is held to the bar of efficacy. If it is not pertinent to the work of the production it is not constructive content. While there is much of interest surrounding the world of the play, playwright, and production, it is only that which will serve the specific production that is the work to dramaturg. If it is presented in a way that is difficult to use, confusing, or too large in scope to be effective, then it really does not matter how good the information may be, it does not serve its function. One of the fundamental skills we develop is to edit our explorations and synthesize the content we find into workable pieces. To dramaturg is to offer usable content in a useful manner.

The Question and Answer Are in the Text

This is an important maxim. While the dramaturg is working on a specific production with all of the particularities created by the assembled company and received by the audience, the dramaturg is also an advocate for the text and its writer. The questions that arise are from the story the playwright crafted, and the clues to the answers are there as well.

Don't Sacrifice Truth for Authenticity

An additional consideration when parsing the questions and answers to dramaturg is the tenuous and fluctuating relationship between authenticity and truth. It is important that we as dramaturgs remember that as much as we ask the questions and provide the content to bring the world of the play and the world of the production into alignment, the precision of the content is a tool, not an end. The purpose of our questions and our answers is to collaborate in the creative process of a performance for an audience. The value of our contribution lies in the effectiveness of what we add to that creative end. Consequently, the truth of the whole is of paramount concern, and there may come the time where that truth has to overshadow the accuracy of the part.

For example, if music is being used to establish a time period, the choice will necessarily be what the audience will hear as the correct time period. If it sounds like the 1920s in a way that will resonate with a contemporary audience, but was actually composed in 1932, the truth of the experience will be more compelling than the accuracy of the date. This is not to say that accuracy and attention to historic and cultural detail is unimportant. However, the appearance of an anachronistic element is arguably more important than an actual anachronism – at least in our stories. It is this understanding, this connection to the end goal of a production for an audience, that shapes the dramaturg's work.

Answer the Question Asked

While the context of the question, the need of the audience, and the purpose of the response are all important, there is a profound aspect that should not be overlooked. The dramaturg needs to answer the question asked. Delving too far into context and subtext removes him from the proximity of the question and he is not serving the purpose to dramaturg. Once again it is about responding to what is there, and unpacking the question. The dramaturg needs to remember that he unpacks the question in order to better provide the answer – to the question asked.

The ability to navigate the question is integral to the development of the mindset to dramaturg. Finding the questions to ask and those to answer, as well as determining how best to do that, is a good starting point. In the process of unpacking the question, there are two important points to keep in mind, the first being to stay connected to the notion of efficacy. One of the reasons that it is sometimes hard to justify the presence of the dramaturg in the room is because a production can happen without someone dedicated to that role. Consequently, it is not considered vital because it is not essential. Opportunity lost is much harder to quantify. However, the presence of a dedicated dramaturg adds so much to a work, in terms of its collaboration, depth and breadth of context, and ultimately provides a more enriching audience experience.

If a question is easily answered and requires merely an internet search that anyone can do, that is not a question that characterizes dramaturgy. From a process standpoint, it is convenient and efficient to have one individual finding and cataloguing the answers to the detail questions – something that often makes it into the casebook – but that is not the creative presence in the production that can be most valuable in a dramaturg. It is not merely the exchange of concrete information that is the result of the questions we are asked, rather the approach and relationship to the questions asked that shows our mindset. The ability to unpack the questions we answer and the ones we ask are key components to approaching dramaturgy.

Dramaturgy is a way of seeing and a manner of engagement. It is an outlook that requires flexibility and dexterity of thought and openness of perspective. It is a way to communicate ideas that is dependent on the target of our communication for its form and content. It is a collation of questions, thoughtfully and creatively presented for our audience. It is a verb that relies on the currency of questions to develop the mindset.

Summary

One of the chief components of the mindset to dramaturg is the ability to ask and answer questions. The dramaturg encounters the question, uncovers its meaning and intent, and finds the most effective way to deliver it. The nature of the question, as well as the means by which it is communicated, is determined by its purpose and its audience.

3

THE FOREST AND THE TREES

The director and dramaturg are meeting to talk about the characters in the play and their relationship to the historical people on whom they are based. This has been a point of concern for the production team as they want to be sure to be true to the source material while at the same time giving actors and designers creative license with character and aesthetic. The director is concerned that too much connection to the "real life" people will cause the actors to create imitations or caricatures in an attempt to recreate them. The dramaturg has a whole series of images, writings, and video of the real people as well as thorough character analyses from the text. The two talk through various options of how to balance the historicism with the artistic needs of the actors, and ultimately come up with a plan. In rehearsal the dramaturg's responsibility is to watch for inaccuracies. Rather than give the actors the context on the real people, he offers a general idea of who they were in conjunction with the character work the actors are doing themselves. Then through the course of the rehearsal he informs the director and the actors when there is something that seems inaccurate or off for the character he is based on. In one case, the person was an avid runner, a detail that had not made it into the script, so when the actor talked about smoking as a bit of business to show the character's anxiety, the dramaturg stepped in. The director and dramaturg agreed that the most useful way to address the relationship between character and person was to watch for inaccuracies since the accuracies would take care of themselves – they were innate in the text and the actors' choices.

The above scenario is notable because it illustrates a particular benefit of the dramaturg's mindset to a production. One of the primary elements of the mindset is to maintain a clear sense of the general picture, the whole production, the story being told, while being able to navigate details. The dramaturg maintains focus on the larger needs of the production while examining the particulars of which it consists.

The idiom "you cannot see the forest for the trees" is particularly appropriate to understand this aspect of dramaturgy. It is a saying that is frequently used to describe a person who is unable to see the "big picture," someone for whom practical steps are clear, while strategy and long-term planning are elusive. For the mindset to dramaturg, the saying has more to offer than merely not seeing the scope of an idea. It speaks to the notion that a person can get so fixated on the details that he loses the ability to see the entire structure those details compose. If the attention becomes too particularly focused on the specific – the trees – there is a risk that the whole production will become unrecognizable to the audience. The distinction here is important: it is not that the whole disappears, rather that it becomes indistinguishable. There is no clarity of "forest" when we get too caught up in the "trees."

While missing the forest for the trees has a negative connotation, however, in the formation of the dramaturg's mindset, it also offers an exciting image for the work. When reversed, it is not so much a snare as an opportunity to develop a point of view that is decidedly double-visioned – forest and trees, as it were. The presence of the dramaturg allows for a specific member of the artistic team to be focused on the big picture, as well as the detail, and to help maintain clarity of both imperatives throughout the production cycle. The big picture, the forest, is the goal for the production and the story that is ultimately told to the audience. When the dramaturg maintains that image in the forefront of her mind, the mindset stays attuned to the general goal of performance alongside the very specific detail of the production elements, acting and directing choices.

Play production is particularly receptive to that point of view since it is vulnerable to the pitfall of getting lost in the detail, as is any complex system. Production is the composite of the collaboration of different artists working in varying disciples, and each discipline itself having a tremendous amount of particulars with which to contend. It is possible to get caught up in the intricacies of the costume design in a way that obscures the certainty that the costume detail is all in support of the clothes characters wear in a particular production of a certain play. These are details that are created in order to join the composition of the visual landscape of the theatrical event. A dramaturg can be a vital part of this process as she maintains sight of the "forest" of the production in order to keep the "trees" of the elements of production from becoming a discrete focus.

The relationship between tree and forest, between part and whole, is an integral relationship for the dramaturg. He needs to be able to respond to the piece without getting lost in it, to discuss the particular without removing it from its context. Once again it is the interrelated nature that is important in the mindset to dramaturg, it is the ability to recognize the composite of trees – to continue with the idiom – as a combination that exists for the revelation of the forest. We examine the specific moments of stage composition and look at the particular artistic choices made throughout the production, and we see them as parts of the mosaic of the theatrical event to be revealed to an audience. It is inextricably connected and it is through that connection we can evaluate the parts; the blocking of the scene is recognizable because it is part of the development of character relationship, the revelation of mood, the topography of the production.

The mindset is developed through the balance of big picture and specific detail. It is not enough that the dramaturg maintains a view of the whole picture; she must also be able to connect to the detail. If she does not understand the workings of the stage composition, she will not be able to recognize when that is the piece that is out of sync. The dramaturg works by seeing the pieces and the whole, by seeing the pieces as the vital composite parts of the whole. In addition, she is able to reflect on the process and reassure collaborators that the production is appropriately affirming both forest and trees.

While forests and trees create a useful image, a more specific way of framing this is that the dramaturg looks at the production holistically. What does it mean to look at something holistically? She sees the parts as intrinsic to the whole, and sees the production as a whole system.

The last chapter touched on the dramaturgical reading of a text as one that considers it as a complete work, read without the filter of any single element of production. This sense of looking at the whole is one part of seeing holistically – being able to see how the composition of elements fit together into the whole script and ultimately the whole production. That is only one facet and the ability to see holistically is a broader perspective that affects every aspect of dramaturgical work. It is the ability to recognize that each element of the production from early drafts of a text through the final dress rehearsal is a piece of the larger work, and to hold the image of the whole in place throughout the process. It is this way of seeing, a manner of engaging with the material that characterizes the work and prevents us from losing sight of the whole.

Seeing the whole is one aspect of seeing. However, the holistic approach also means recognizing that the whole is not just the combination of the parts. A holistic look is the understanding that the parts are interconnected and only recognizable in relation to the whole. When we look at a script, a rehearsal, an event, we seek to understand it as a whole system that exists because of the interrelated pieces in a particular arrangement – and those pieces exist for that composition.

It is not merely the revelation that the parts make up the whole, or even that the whole is more than the sum of its parts. The additional conceptual step for a holistic viewpoint relates to the pieces themselves, and offers a corollary to the idiom of forests and trees. In order to practice a holistic way of seeing and get into the mindset to dramaturg, we must also be diligent and avoid "not seeing the trees for the forest." The notion is not as effective turned around, yet it does hint at the pitfall of being too "big picture." If we become so fixated on the whole that we become unable to see how the parts are constructed, we become less effective to dramaturg. The pieces are explicable in relation to the whole in the same way that the composition of the pieces reveals the whole. Thus the "trees" are as likely to be missed as the "forest" and the goal of dramaturgy is to see holistically and keep both in clear view.

For example, the sound design does not stand alone, it is explicable as a part of the complete production and so the dramaturg is able to consider it discretely in terms of response to the sound itself, but is also grounded in the understanding that it is existentially connected to the larger story. The music that is chosen has characteristics that will offer a commentary on the action, and a holistic point of view will see the effectiveness of the music itself alongside its contribution to the overall mood of the scene and the larger style of the production.

The mindset to dramaturg is a way of engaging with material. It is an expansive outlook that enables us to question, respond, and be creative collaborators. One of the places this mindset is formed is in the approach to material. The way that a dramaturg approaches a subject is a significant part of what determines how he responds to it, and an open and flexible response is the result of a clear and nimble approach. Clear and nimble, specific and flexible, effective and creative; while these are not specifically contradictory ideas, they do require a kind of deftness to hold the balance. That balance is what we are talking about with dramaturg as a mindset. Seeing as a dramaturg prepares one to hold that balance and to be an effective member of a creative team. Thus, the way to maintain and expand the flexible thinking of dramaturgy is to train oneself to see holistically.

Script reading as a dramaturg is well suited to a holistic outlook. While the dramaturg refines his skills at script analysis and seeks to be conversant in genre, style, and structure he also looks at each individual element of the playwright's work as something woven into the play and inextricably linked to its entirety. Consequently, talking about the text, even when focusing on a seemingly discrete element of the piece, he stays vigilant to the truth of the whole. As discussed in the previous chapter, whether it is thought, the spine, or the theme, the overall meaning of the play, the idea of the play that will be exhibited in the production, is something that the dramaturg clarifies early on. Throughout the production cycle, then, he is vigilant in helping to maintain that production idea. Character, action, language, time, place, metaphor, rhythm, theme; none of these things has a meaningful independent existence, so one consciously examines the element as part of the composition and its determined meaning.

For example, the strength of characterization shown through action and language is an important building block of a playwright's creation, and the way to look at those clues of characterization is completely case-dependent. The manner in which Troy Maxson is constructed in August Wilson's *Fences* is reliant on the specificity of the world Wilson creates, and is assessed and critiqued based on that world's internal mechanisms. It is not a simple equation of "action and language reveals character" in and of itself. When Troy tells his son that he cannot play football for a college recruiter, there is a whole psychological element to the character that offers insight to that moment. However, there is also mid-century America and the character backstory provided by Wilson that makes that moment mean something different with that character than it would in another circumstance. The construction of character does not happen without context, and the dramaturgical read of the assemblage of the character of Troy is by necessity affixed to its existence within *Fences* specifically and that is how we engage with it.

Similarly, rhythm in and of itself has little significance, but the rhythm of the language of Maria Irene Fornes is integral to experiencing her work. She explores different styles in her plays, and Fornes often writes about people trying to educate themselves and change their circumstances, such as in the stark and bleak work *Mud*. The rhythm of her language, word and silence, is revelatory and a key to understanding her worlds. Once again, it is experienced as part of the larger work, and understood through that connection; rhythm is a tool of analysis not of itself, but of the whole play.

The relationship to the elements of a thing as inextricably linked to the thing itself carries over throughout the dramaturgical activity. When working with a playwright, a production team, responding in rehearsal or preparing materials for the audience, the dramaturgical mindset relies on the ability to hold in mind the larger picture, the whole as well as the part(s). Once again this whole is the overall thought of the text and the overall goal of the production. The dramaturg tries to keep the idea of the whole piece in mind while she asks and answers questions, and it further shapes the way she addresses any given aspect of production, each conversation with each collaborator. Every piece of the production is treated as part of the whole, and is not dealt with in a way that removes it from that essential function. The conversations about the specific imagery in the language spoken are steeped in the context of how it fits into the play as a whole. While all of the production team seeks to keep the individual parts connected to the whole production, it is a primary function of dramaturgy to be sure the production as a whole stays linked to the individual parts.

The dramaturgical read of a text or a situation is one that is both holistic and open; we as dramaturgs strive to meet the work on its own terms without the bias of personal expectation. An additional part of this openness is that we do not limit our focus to any individual element of production and so are able to see how all of the pieces interconnect. We see from the start that a piece can be framed in order to discuss it with specificity, but that piece does not have an identity autonomous from the whole from which it is lifted. This connection is important to maintain and the understanding is vital to developing the mindset to dramaturg. The response we offer comes from our understanding of context, and that starts with the whole play/production/event as the context to any single aspect of it.

The ability to ask questions and offer context for individual aspects of text and particular elements of production is one of the roles of the dramaturg, and this also requires the capacity to look at the distinct element and understand its particular composition. It is important that we keep the image of the whole in mind – that we remember that each element is part of a whole production – however, we also need the clarity to consider the individual components themselves.

The key is to maintain the balance between the pieces and the whole, between the trees and the forest. The individual elements do not have an autonomous meaning – a costume piece out of the context of the production for which it is designed is not of consequence from a dramaturgical or theatrical perspective. It takes on a particular dramaturgical relevance when it becomes part of the visual landscape of a specific production. It is the interrelationship of production element to production that is significant and is the place we focus on when seeking the mindset to dramaturg. We need to be able to see the individual element clearly, and what we see is its particular composition as it relates to the whole production. The one does not exist without the other, forest and trees exist both simultaneously and inextricably.

It is useful to take a moment to distinguish how the holistic perspective of the dramaturg differs from the director's point of view. As stated earlier, the nature and practice of that relationship depends on the people involved, and the overlap in roles will vary greatly depending on the nature of the process. However, there is a particular distinction that can be made between the two roles when it comes to holistic seeing. While the director is also looking at all the component parts in order to create the cohesive whole – whatever that may be artistically and stylistically – her point of view is one to figure out how those pieces fit together. The dramaturg looks with the somewhat objective perspective of an external audience member, with the insider knowledge of a creative collaborator. She does not need to figure out how they work together; she responds to their assembly as, "Do they work together?"

She represents the audience throughout the creative process, and provides that lens to collaborators. Again, the dramaturg sees without the limiting filter of a single production element, so she has the luxury to look at the effectiveness of each element and how the elements construct the whole composition.

How do dramaturgs keep the balance? How do they manage not to lose sight of forest or trees? The first step is to acknowledge that the link between part and whole is binding, and consequently any discussion of the one necessarily takes into account the other. It requires embracing the holistic viewpoint and allowing that to guide the dramaturgical work throughout the process. When the dramaturg is seeing holistically and engaging with the material in that manner, she can shape how questions are asked and information is shared in a way that is useful to the project.

Once again the idea of useful and effective comes up, and it is worth reiterating that the process of dramaturgy is about usage and efficacy. Both of these terms have particular resonance in the mindset as they have different objects. The idea of useful indicates the tool itself is able to be put to good effect. Effective, on the other hand, deals with the effect of the usage – the tool was successful in its intended purpose. A dramaturgical mindset allows for practices that are useful to the process and effective in their output. The motivating force that drives process and output is its usefulness in the project, and the outcome is shaped by attention to the effectiveness of its reception. These are encapsulated in the holistic viewpoint, a perspective that creates an effective mindset from which to work. It demands an openness that inspires flexible thinking, as well as a clarity that allows for authentic response.

Flexible thinking is essential in creative collaboration. A dramaturg needs to be open to other ideas and input as well as to constantly find new ways to understand and share context. The holistic approach naturally inspires flexible thinking since each process is unique to that production. If there is not a predictable and fixed process then there is not a standard method the dramaturg uses. The dramaturg needs to be skilled enough to understand the components and how they function and the interpersonal relationship with the artists. She needs to be nimble enough to see how those parts and artists function in different ways for different ends. The openness to the difference and the subsequent flexibility allow for new solutions, creative communication, and more effective collaboration. It is another illustration of how coming into the project with as few presumptions as possible enables a kind of clarity of vision that is crucial to the mindset to dramaturg.

Seeing holistically also establishes a strong foundation for authentic response from the dramaturg. The idea of an authentic response is to be able to engage with what is seen; taking the work on its own terms rather than shaped by expectations or bias. The questions and comments are for the work as presented, not as anticipated, and that clarity of response offers the most to the collaboration. When the dramaturg is genuinely seeing something based on its own construction, recognizing the identity it presents as well as the reality of its composite elements, it gives him the most opportunity for authentic response. To reflect and respond to what is there.

What does a holistic way of seeing look like in practice? How is it connected to the dramaturgical work in a way that makes it an essential part of the mindset?

In Script Reading

When reading a text, the questions of style and form, given circumstances, characterization, rhythm and metaphor are all part of the initial – and ongoing – familiarization with the script. The dramaturg reads with an eye to structure and composition, word choice and tempo. He looks at how the pieces of the text comprise a performable play. As discussed earlier, a dramaturgical read is distinctive because it is not reading for a purpose such as set design or character creation. It is a read that attempts to take the script as a whole work, a blueprint for performance.

What makes a read holistic in approach is that the image of the text as a complete script is kept in mind while looking at the elements of analysis. In addition, the elements themselves are seen as inextricable from the whole, so are defined by their presence in this text. The word choice is not removed from the context of what it conveys but is discussed *as* that context. Characterization has no theoretical existence; it is defined by the character it reveals in this particular play. Every element is revealed by and through its contribution to the whole script. The holistic viewpoint reminds us to stay focused on the connections and not lose sight of the end goal of a text for performance. It also gives us a vocabulary to use in script analysis. Our authentic response to the text is formed with the dialogue that connects the words on the page to the essentials of a play.

A key to reading holistically is allowing the play to reveal the rules of the play. The training and practice in critical analysis is a vital tool, and one gets more facile at recognizing cues and trends. However, the mindset seeks an open view on each work and uses the critical analysis as a structure and vocabulary to apply after the voice of the text is revealed rather than as a way to assess it. In other words, these are diagnostic tools and they provide a way to talk about the play once a person is oriented to it, rather than being a prescription for that orienting. If the play is read based on the expectation of a structure or style, a reader may try to impose that expectation or be critical of ways in which it seemed to fall short. When a play is read as itself, and the structure and style come from the cues the playwright includes, then the dramaturg is getting acquainted with the whole, with the forest of the play.

The dramaturg is reading a new play, and the first time through he is reading with an eye for story and character. He is introduced to the players of the text and goes with them through the events that make up the story. He underlines each word or line that he finds surprising so he has a record of that "first time hearing it" experience which will likely be useful in later rehearsals. He notices character word-choice and action, the descriptions in the stage directions as well as those that the other characters offer. He considers how the story is revealed throughout the text, how time and place are treated, and how the pieces form the whole.

> TIP: *The first time you read a play, make a note of the moments of surprise, delight, confusion, so you can refer back to the first response.*

Each of these elements can be a pivotal point in the production, and the open mindset allows the dramaturg to both see and share it. For example, a reading of Paula Vogel's *How I Learned to Drive* reveals how important the treatment of time can be to revealing character. The play is structured in a series of episodes, framed by driving lessons, and a non-linear chronology. This structure is vital as the response to the pivotal character of Uncle Peck is dependent on the initial ambiguity of the relationship. That ambiguity would not be possible with a chronological telling. The detail of time is foundational to the whole of this play, a circumstance that is dependent on its relationship between structure and story revealed by the rules of the play.

This aspect of the mindset is looking particularly at production dramaturgy with a given script, though the idea of an open and flexible entry point into any kind of source material is fundamental to the holistic point of view and a primary characteristic of the mindset to dramaturg.

With a Playwright

The working dynamic of playwright and dramaturg is completely reliant on the relationship forged between the artists. How the relationship operates is dependent on a number of factors, some personal and stylistic, and others that reflect the process of development. When a dramaturg is working with a playwright on a new work that is in development, the kinds of questions and input he offers is different than when working on a second production. New play development often translates into revisions of the text as part of the process and the dramaturgical work can include helping the playwright to find the shape of the piece. In this context, the ability to clearly discuss the details of the text while understanding where it fits in the whole script is what makes the collaboration effective for the playwright. When we understand what the playwright is trying to accomplish and we can clearly see and respond to what is presented, we are better equipped to ask the questions that will prove useful.

Example:

The dramaturg and playwright talk about the use of musical terminology and accuracy in the piece during a play development process leading up to a public reading. The musical elements are approximate, they offer the mood and tone the playwright seeks, but are not totally authentic for the period. The two have had this conversation twice already and the playwright is pushing back against the dramaturg's growing insistence that the accuracy of the musical references is imperative. The script development is effectively halted as it gets stuck on the point. The playwright grows frustrated and the dramaturg impatient and both become fixated on this device and that dominates the day's work. Time is lost and the collaboration is strained, somewhat, because the mechanism took precedence over the play.

The situation above indicates a scenario where both playwright and dramaturg get caught up in the detail of a production element in a way that stalls the process of the script development. The dramaturg's responsibility to the whole was not met in this scenario and he needs to refocus on the goal of the process. The musical accuracy is undoubtedly important to the play; however, the fixation on that detail will not serve the goal of the process, which is a public reading of the play. In addition, the conflict can ultimately hurt the process as it can strain the relationship between playwright and dramaturg. That is not to imply that new play dramaturgy should be without conflict or disagreement – the dramaturg's role is not useful if it is only a source of agreement – but the holistic point of view can recognize the relative importance of the musical accuracy in relation to the reading of the play.

The "forest" when working with a playwright extends beyond the given text, and this is another aspect of a holistic approach that proves valuable. When a dramaturg works with a playwright she is collaborating with a person and a body of work, not just a single text. The work that happens on a script or in a production feeds back into the subsequent work for the artists involved and that is why script development can also be thought of as playwright development. This is also why it is particularly important to form the relationship and collaboration into something useful and productive that may contribute something valuable to an artistic career. Though this is not done at the neglect of the specific text, it is another illustration of forest and trees.

TIP: Remember that working on a new play is investing in the future of the form.

When it is a long-standing collaboration, the commitment to the body of work is a natural step since the artists have worked on multiple pieces. However, even the first piece they work on has a life cycle that reminds them that this is not an isolated piece. They have the iterations of the script, the questions, and the conversations that end up in varying degrees in the eventual production. The other things the playwright has written are ideally part of the shared knowledge and the dramaturg can see how this piece fits in the writer's career to date, sees this as part of the whole. If she works on an early iteration of a new play with a writer, she is finding the breath of this play, but it is a play that is part of a career that is part of a theatrical moment. This awareness does not result in the dramaturg's mindset being less specific on the single play; it clarifies this single play as a part of something larger, too. In practical terms, it reminds the dramaturg that the conversations and questions will be part of this process, and can also influence the subsequent work.

With a Director

As with the playwright, the efficacy of the dramaturgical process is largely dependent on the relationship established with the director. Clear communication and a specific understanding of the nature of the collaboration are paramount to this relationship. After that, things like style and temperament and the artistic vision can determine how smoothly the process will go; though not to imply smooth is necessarily a more effective mode of artistic collaboration. The holistic dramaturgical mindset can offer a director a perspective that emphasizes the ultimate presence of the audience. This is, of course, the significant source of concentration for the director and while he is composing the production in meeting and rehearsal, he can rely on the additional outlook of the dramaturg. The holistic viewpoint keeps keen focus on the elements of production coming together as well as the outline of the shape they will ultimately make and can voice a concern if those things start to diverge.

There is definite overlap between how a director and dramaturg look at a text and a process. Both have "big picture" perspectives and are committed to how the text for performance becomes the production for the audience. In the director-led model, it is the director's vision and the execution of that vision that ultimately shapes the production, it is she who works with actors and articulates a vision for designers. The dramaturg's work supports that of the director. He seeks material, asks questions, and shares ideas in order to help sharpen the director's vision and shape the clarity of the story being told.

The dramaturg brings his analysis of the text and his understanding of the context of its creation into conversation with the director, who has her own analysis and understanding. This allows for useful conversation about vision and execution. The dramaturg can ask informed questions about the implications and associations and help the director look at her choices from multiple perspectives. Then throughout the process the dramaturg has his continued contextual understanding joined with his firsthand knowledge of the director's goals and experience of the work in rehearsal. This unique perspective, intimate understanding without the limits of a production element to execute, creates an extremely useful ally for a director. While the director ultimately needs to create the world of the production, the collaboration with a dramaturg who is also looking at the whole production from the beginning will enable a more cohesive vision.

In Production Meetings

Production meetings are perhaps the clearest example of the need to consider the work holistically. While the dramaturg does not typically have a functional role in the production meeting in the same way as designers and management, she is in the room to further her understanding of the intent of the collaborators as well as offer input to the creative process where it may be useful. The production meeting is an opportunity to hear the status of the various elements of production as well as be available for conversations that arise regarding artistic elements. Understanding the goals of the production creates a better understanding of how the elements fit together and provides a foundation from which to ask questions and offer insight into the process. While each collaborator is looking toward the final production for the audience, the dramaturg is able to do so with a specialized point of view. She can keep clear focus on the manner in which the pieces fit together and how they are converging toward the goals of the production without the need to track any single element or solve any specific challenge.

What does a dramaturg do in production meetings? This is a common question, and once again has a situation-dependent answer to some degree. However, there are two fundamental roles he plays in the meetings: to listen to others and to represent the holistic perspective when called upon.

The dramaturg is in the production meetings to hear what is said, to be present for the conversations about ideas and aesthetics. As things develop and change, he is in the room to know how the production process continues to develop, to know what to look for in terms of content he generates as well as what he is watching for in rehearsal. He is there to listen for the continuity in idea and goal for the production. The production meeting is when the conceptual framework for the production is typically discussed, and how the various elements of production will fit together. Since the dramaturg is attentive to that fit, those are conversations in which he is particularly invested. He can also be an advocate for discussions in a way that will stop potential misunderstanding or conflicting direction among elements from happening.

TIP: Best idea in the room wins.

The direct answer to the question, "What does a dramaturg do in production meetings?" He listens, asks questions, ensures the director's vision is clearly understood and stays informed on the development of the production. He keeps sight of the end goal of a performance for an audience and helps to make sure everyone is working on the same production.

With Designers, Technicians, and Management

The production meeting is the place in which the overall conversations and updates happen; however, that is not the sole contact the dramaturg has with designers, technicians and management. She can be a content resource for designers and technicians, and vice versa. All members of the artistic team conduct some kinds of research and that can be a shared resource or a point of connection in conversation, as well as common source of materials that can ultimately go to actors and to audience.

Once again, the clarity and flexibility of the holistic approach provides a beneficial response to the production work. The dramaturg is connected to the needs of the production in process, while also keeping in mind the future audience for the production. This will inform the kinds of questions to ask or answer with designers and technicians and shapes the way the dramaturg presents context. The context needed for the process of getting a show built is better steered by the knowledge of what the audience will need from that build. It is the holistic viewpoint that gives the dramaturg a vantage point from which to contribute to the technical aspects of the show as well. It is the understanding of how the pieces work in concert and the ability to respond to those pieces clearly and authentically that characterize effective dramaturgy.

Part of the "trees" the dramaturg sees in the composition of the "forest" of the production is the unique process of designers. Understanding the language and the specific challenges of theatrical design are vital to being an effective collaborator with designers and technicians. He does not need to be able to design a set, but the dramaturg needs to understand the point of view of the scenic designer in order to be a useful collaborator. When he can speak to composition and flow, as well as the conceptual cues of the landscape of the production, he will be more suited to offer effective material as well as a useful point of view. He can offer direct input as well when details of the design are worked out, such as what kind of furniture for Chekhov's *Three Sisters* can reveal time, place, status, and action. The dramaturg can offer his contextual understanding of the world of the play to join the designer's contextual and aesthetic ideas to help that designer come up with a successful selection.

The effectiveness of communication is paramount in these relationships. The director is responsible for the cohesiveness of the production, so it is her vision to which the aesthetic and technical elements need to align. Consequently, the dramaturg is a useful sounding board as well as resource when he is clear and up-to-date on the director's ideas.

In Rehearsal

The dramaturg in rehearsal acts as a resource, creative collaborator, and surrogate for the audience and all of these roles are improved through a holistic way of seeing. The value of authentic response is greatest here, where she can offer director and actors a reflective commentary on the work being done. This is where listening and participating in production meetings pays off. Continuing to focus on the connection between the elements of production and the goal for the production allows the dramaturg to help navigate that process, through questions asked and answered. Again, removed from the need to come up with a solution, she is able to offer a response to what she sees in a way that gives the artistic collaborators more information about what is presented.

In rehearsal the dramaturg watches for continuity and specificity within the production. She is watching with an eye to what the audience will ultimately see and so looking for the strength of the constructed narrative. Her role in the rehearsal changes throughout the production cycle, and will be discussed in more detail in Chapter 7. However, the overall arc of rehearsal involvement is as follows. She offers a context presentation at the first rehearsal and helps facilitate the discussion after the first read-through. She listens to the read-through. She makes note of the surprising moments as well as the points in the play that affect the mood of the room. She listens for rhythm and pace as well as any clues to the moments in the play that will offer a particular challenge for cast or audience. For example, if there is a scene that seems to get monotonous in the reading, that may indicate the need for special attention to energy and pace in the staging. Or if there is a significant plot point that is immersed in a fast-paced conversation, this will be a necessary marker for the audience and something to note from the start of the process. In addition, if members of the cast respond to something in the play with discomfort or uncertainty, or seem to have a strong resonance, that will be an indication for the dramaturg to look for specific content to support the cast in those subjects and moments.

The most direct interaction with the full ensemble happens in the early days of the rehearsal process, the read-through and table work when there is discussion about the play and the production and some initial choices are made and explored. Once the process moves into staging the play the dramaturg's role becomes less visible in some ways, though no less important. She watches how the actor's choices and director's compositions fulfill the story of the play and the goals of the production. Throughout the staging rehearsals and the run-throughs, the dramaturg is watching and listening, bringing in materials in support of the questions raised and ideas explored, and offering the director a holistic point of view on the work at each phase of the process.

When the production goes into technical rehearsals and (possible) previews, the dramaturg is in the room watching, listening, asking and answering questions as needed, and continues to look at what the audience will see – to look holistically at the production and its elements. He looks with attention on what has transpired alongside the knowledge of what was intended. In addition, this final phase helps solidify what kinds of audience outreach and contact will be most useful.

One of the most effective ways to dramaturg in rehearsal is to offer a responsive point of view, to tell the director what she sees and provide that perspective from which to proceed. The questions asked and answered are valuable contributions to the rehearsal process, and when those can be supplemented with a clear vision of what is happening on stage, the dramaturgy is its most useful and effective. Sometimes the best thing to offer is, "She tells him it's over and she stands there and he says he is sorry and walks across the room." All that is doing is describing the action of a moment, and it will likely enable the director to see why a scene felt unclear. While the director is focusing on the "trees" of blocking, stage business, characterization and tempo, a dramaturg can watch for the "forest" of the story told in the room.

Some things a dramaturg does in rehearsal:

- be the advocate for the playwright;
- provide the eye of an audience;
- watch for continuity;
- answer content questions;
- offer perspective on cultural/social practices within the play;
- watch for character consistency and clarity;
- ask and answer questions of and from the director;
- look for specific moment/idea if requested;
- take notes on flow, pace, overall rhythm of performance;
- verify historical/cultural practices, watch for accuracy;
- keep rehearsal notes, staying up to speed on process and schedule;
- watch where focus is drawn on stage.

It is impossible to come up with a comprehensive list of what a dramaturg does in rehearsal since it is completely dependent on the show and the relationship. The most accurate statement would be that she dramaturgs in rehearsal. She looks at the needs of the rehearsal and provides context for that work. She pays close attention to how all of the pieces are coming together to form the production the director seeks. She listens and watches, offers content and asks questions, she sees the forest and the trees.

Non-Production

The examples offered here are particular to the production dramaturg in a somewhat traditional collaboration with a fixed script. However, when we talk about dramaturg as mindset we automatically include projects outside the traditional theatre. Dramaturgy as mindset is a way of seeing the world and engaging with material, and when a dramaturg is working, the only definitive commonality is that she is defining a process in order to collaborate effectively. Whether this happens in another performance and/or storytelling form or something entirely different in scope and mode, the dramaturg is aided by the practice of seeing holistically. Whatever the project, when we as dramaturgs are able to see it as a composite of individual pieces that are knowable through their relationship to the whole we are more able to think flexibly and offer authentic response to what we encounter.

The ability to see the big picture and to think strategically in terms of how the parts work together is something that is useful in any collaborative endeavor. The holistic point of view, and even more so, the open, responsive perspective makes the dramaturgical mindset particularly appealing. The dramaturg responds to what he sees, not what he expected or hoped, but has an informed framework from which to mirror what he sees. He can offer a point of view about the efficacy of what is there without the filter of what he thinks should be there.

This chapter conjures the saying "cannot see the forest for the trees" as a way of understanding a holistic viewpoint as essential to the dramaturgical mindset. A strong sense of where we are going and the ability to recognize the markers along the way is the foundation of effective dramaturgy. In addition, the facility with which one can recognize the markers as inextricably linked to the *where* becomes characteristic of the mindset. We seek the forest and trees with clarity and creative honesty that provide the context for a useful collaboration and artistic offering.

Summary

The ability to see both the details and the larger picture of a situation is an integral part of the mindset to dramaturg. The perspective is shaped by seeing the way the particular artistic elements form together to construct the narrative.

4

TIMING IS EVERYTHING

A dramaturg and director are talking after rehearsal at the beginning of run-throughs at the end of the fourth week of a six-week rehearsal period. The actors are off book, the blocking is solid and the character relationships are firmly established on stage. The dramaturg has questions about the tempo of the piece and has found commentary from the playwright about the rhythmic influences that the dramaturg feels are important aspects to include to get the feel the writer is going for; also, the rhythm of the language is important to the structure of the narrative. The dramaturg has well-formed questions and valuable material to share – that she found and formulated three weeks previously. However, she knows that the start of the second week is much too soon to talk about rhythm so she holds off. At the end of week four, she is given the go-ahead by the director to work with the actors on rhythmic exercises that positively affect the tempo of the play and bring to light the various influences the playwright alluded to.

The most important contribution a dramaturg can make to a production is attention and useful and timely input. To dramaturg is an activity that is completely present, engaged, and in the moment. The usefulness of the response that a dramaturg offers is inextricably connected to the when she offers it; consequently, it is vital she is immersed in the given moment of the process and utilizes opportunities to communicate with director, actors, and eventually the audience. In the same way that she needs to stay connected to both forest and trees as discussed in the previous chapter, the mindset of the dramaturg is formed by the close attention to the point in time of the moment, with an eye to the whole arc of the production schedule.

The dramaturg constantly looks for the opportunity to provide valuable input and response, and it is the nuanced understanding of when to bring them to the collaborators that determines their ultimate usefulness. This can come about only with close attention to the people and process of the production. The dramaturg needs to understand the scope of the project and have a general idea of what goes into each given element in order to be attuned to the schedule of events. In addition, the dramaturg's pre-production work often includes a thoughtful analysis of the timeline of the dramaturgy in order to coincide with the timeline of the production.

There are a variety of circumstances that affect the schedule of events both in the particular elements of production and the project as a whole. While the dramaturg does not need the kind of intimate and detailed knowledge of workflow that a production manager or stage manager requires, he is well served by following the general schedule of the production so he knows when the various pieces are at which stage of development. Again, it is not necessary that a dramaturg knows every aspect of production in minute detail, but he should understand the various processes and overall timeline and maintain them throughout the production, while exercising flexibility in response to changes. The more he understands about the process of production, the better he can navigate the terrain of a production in construction.

The schedule of events is also determined by the preference of the artistic team and the demands of the show. In every show there are fixed points such as the dates of performance, when the show will be loaded into the theatre, and marketing deadlines, among others. These are the built-ins for timing; however, the dramaturg needs to be in contact with collaborators for the particulars of the process. There is the lead time the costume designer likes to have for his research before preliminary designs and when the set designer prefers to finalize her painter's elevations. There is the manner in which the director does individual character work and how quickly she blocks the show. In addition, the needs of the show will also drive timing – the movement for a Restoration piece like Congreve's *Way of the World* requires rehearsal time spent on the physical work of the period movement, rehearsal time that would be used in a different way in staging a modern work.

The dramaturg takes this timeline and incorporates it into her mind-set. The mindset to dramaturg is predicated on relationships, and this is another example of the value of strong points of connection through-out the collaborative team so the dramaturg knows where in their own processes designers, actors, and technicians are at various points in time. The purpose of this knowledge and attention is to have the most complete view of the varying pieces of the production. Think about the dramaturg's process as a system of moving parts; at different times in the production one wants to be able to look at one aspect and know where it is in terms of its own trajectory and its construction into the whole project. In order to know what she is looking at as well as gauge what input is most useful for a collaborator, the dramaturg needs to know where those elements are in the general and specific produc-tion schedule and be able to track that schedule in relation to her own particular perspective.

Attention is closely aligned with timing, because understanding how the pieces come together necessarily includes their sequence and their time frame. Knowing the timing of all the processes and how they overlap and connect enables the dramaturg to recognize when and where is appropriate for what she brings to the collaboration. To be effective, it is often the "when" a question is asked or a point raised that becomes at least as important as the "what" and "how" something is addressed. Sometimes the willingness to listen to a collaborator work through a question is incredibly helpful, and the role as a trusted and knowledgeable resource invested in the overall success of the produc-tion is a good place from which to listen. This comes from being attentive and in the moment of the production. Timing is integral to the effectiveness of the dramaturg's work.

It is worth noting that the dramaturg deals with his own scheduled deadlines within the production calendar.

- A presentation for the designers is made early in the process to introduce contextual material.
- A presentation at the first read-through for the actors, and at this time the actor's packet, in whatever form that takes, is made available.
- Audience outreach materials and press releases have their own deadlines, as do study guides and program notes.

- Guests that the dramaturg invites to speak to cast or audience need to be scheduled in advance and when they are both feasible and useful.

The dramaturgical tasks are subject to the production schedule and the work follows a timeline in the same way as the other production elements.

Dramaturgy has another relationship to timing outside the production timeline; the dramaturg determines the timing of the questions he asks and input he offers. The timing of their delivery largely shapes the questions asked and answered, as discussed in the previous chapter. "When" matters at least as much as "how," and how useful the work is will be directly related to it happening at the right time.

When to Ask the Question

One fundamental aspect of timing for the dramaturg is deceptively simple – when does he ask the question that may change the trajectory of the production? This is the most apparent element of timing in dramaturgy, the issue of when to offer input. As mentioned, the knowledge of the process of the project as well as the practice of the collaborating artists are both important contributors to determining the timing answer. It is similar to the vital skill of a director – knowing when to give a note. For the director, the challenge is recognizing when the note will be most effective, when it will be usable by the actor. However, although similar, the question has more clarity for the director since giving notes is a clear and expected aspect of the job, so finding the when and how to make them most effective is part of the exchange between director and actor.

The timing question for the dramaturg is somewhat more complicated, as the specificity of the role of questioner is not as clear, and the dramaturg is also trying to build trust and deepen relationships. Consequently, it is of even more importance that timing be considered. A director may give a note at a less effective time but that will not call into question his right to give a note. On the other hand, a poorly timed question from the dramaturg early in the process may affect the future overall reception of the dramaturg, particularly in a new collaboration, and may call into doubt the usefulness of the role. This is why the care of the pre-production work and the close attention to timing and process is so important, to help the dramaturg avoid or recover from a timing misstep. Dramaturgy is only as useful as it is effective, so the importance of timing is not to be underestimated. Combined with the mindset, relationships are as closely connected to the sequence of events as they are to their composition.

So when does the dramaturg ask the question? Easily said, the short and easy answer is to ask the question when it will be the most useful to the project. However, what makes it useful and deciding when that will be the case is the real challenge for the dramaturg.

Close attention to process and useful observation of the collaborators helps the dramaturg contribute questions at opportune times. A question is going to be effective if the asking and/or the answer will inform some element of the project. That happens when it is pertinent and when it is heard. It does not matter how useful a question may be if the people who need to engage with it are unable to hear it. Thus the first consideration is to recognize if the group is at a point at which the collaborators are able to hear the question.

Hearing the question has a literal component – is it asked in a time and place in which we have the attention of our intended recipient? Too often something may be brushed aside because it is lost in a casual mention or among too many other things that require more immediate attention. Similarly, it needs to be asked in a way that makes sense to the collaborator. It seems as if this would happen automatically; however, depending on the circumstances of the asking, it can be out of a context that makes sense to him and consequently be lost for that reason. For example, if a question that pertains to characterization is brought up in the midst of a meeting about the set design, the likelihood that the question will be heard is significantly lower than it would be at a point in which he is thinking about characters.

Another way in which the idea of hearing it is important relates to the manner in which it is presented. If the question is asked in a way that seems to be a criticism rather than an inquiry, the natural response is to "push back," particularly when it is early in the process and ideas and details are being developed. Even if the intent of the dramaturg is legitimately to ask the question to spark the conversation that will help the collaboration, he risks shutting down that process by presenting a poorly phrased – and poorly timed – apparent criticism of the work. The attention that he exercises also necessarily includes the way a question is received in order for it to be heard.

The Question Itself

Finally, the form in which the question is presented directly affects the likelihood of its reception. One of the first things a dramaturg does after joining a production team is to establish with a collaborator how best to communicate. There are some directors who will want questions only in writing so they can read and think about them at their preferred time of day. There are playwrights who want only to talk directly after a rehearsal or designers whose preferred place of conversation is outside the scene shop on lunch breaks. When these modes of communication are established up front, it makes the process of asking questions much easier and the dramaturg is able to avoid a potential misstep. These preferred ways need to be coordinated with the dramaturg's own preferences and strengths; it is not a single-direction communication. When he is able to work within the expectations and comfort of collaborators, the dramaturg has more room to ask questions that provoke thought and conversation. When the dramaturg wants to be heard and have the most effect, he makes sure that he asks the question at the most opportune time and in the most appropriate manner.

Timing lets the question be heard, and it also determines the pertinence of the question. The process of the entire project and its component parts has a particular order and flow that will allow for questions to be useful at particular times. The dramaturg is closely connected to the flow of the process for precisely this reason, so he knows where to place questions that will be useful. While a designer is gathering a general visual style, a question about the particulars of a texture would not be pertinent; however, in the midst of a build a question about texture can be incredibly enlightening.

A question about stage composition and its relationship to character relationship is a really useful conversation to have in week four. At this point, character choices are formed and stage pictures are solidifying. The rehearsals are including run-throughs and the story narrative is starting to take a strong shape. The dramaturg can ask the director about intent and have a conversation about shape and meaning in a way that can support the work of the director and be productive to the production. This is a conversation that would be not useful in earlier rehearsals when character is not established and the blocking is largely exploratory.

When to Ask It Again

Frustrating for the dramaturg, there will be times in which the question is pertinent, clearly presented at a useful time, and heard – to no visible effect. So the attention to timing becomes important once more when it is addressing the challenge of when to ask a question again. This concern consists of the same issues already mentioned, though heightened, since it is reintroducing a point and the dramaturg does not want to come across as argumentative.

To ask again, the fundamental process is the same; watch for a time when the question can be asked again, when it will be heard and when it is effective to the creative process. These circumstances are partially affected by the reason it needs to be asked again. If the original question was disregarded, then the need is to find another way to present it to the recipient where it may be applicable. If the person being asked did not see the need to engage with the question asked, the next step is looking for another approach that will highlight the importance. Manner and timing are vital in this case where the collaborator could feel harassed or berated by a repetition and so less apt to explore it. Consequently, how the question is phrased and presented needs to be crafted in a way that is both new and constructive. In addition, the question is asked where it is useful in the production schedule and the dramaturg has a limited window of time to affect the play. Asking questions that may inform materials after things have been bought and design elements are under construction is not useful and can conceivably give the impression that the dramaturg is unfamiliar or unconcerned with the practicality of the designer's and technician's work. In that circumstance, the conversation around the question should not happen, to avoid damaging a relationship, which could have a lasting effect on future collaboration.

Timing can help to preserve the collaboration while the dramaturg makes another attempt with the question. She needs to ensure that the recipient has had enough time to process what was asked as well as stay close enough to the original asking so there is no doubt that all parties know this is something that is asked again; she should not try to mask that fact. The specific time period that incorporates both of these needs is not fixed and depends on the nature and context of the question. For example, if the development question is about the overarching metaphor that is interwoven into many aspects of the production, the dramaturg likely has a broader range of opportunities to ask the specific question. Also, when the subject matter is part of other conversations, there is typically a greater willingness to explore it via additional avenues. At the same time, if the question is about a particular bit of stage business, the dramaturg may want to ask the question again before it becomes practiced and fixed and more strongly associated with a character or a moment, while also leaving enough room for the collaborators to see what that bit of business is offering the scene and have a context with which to think about the question.

There are times when the question is asked again because the issue has arisen anew, and this requires a slightly different approach to the question of when. If the question comes up in another context, it can be addressed as soon as the circumstances are amenable – when it is useful and when it will be heard – and the pitfall to avoid is the appearance of looking for the opportunity to ask the question again. That is to say, while the question that was dismissed may appear to be berating when it is brought up again, when the question is one that was addressed and has arisen again, it may appear to be badgering when it comes up for a second time. Avoid the "gotcha" appearance, because that is the element that causes the most direct harm to collaboration. The result of this kind of conflict is often the impression that "being right" takes precedence over the needs of the project, and that is a circumstance that shuts down the artistic alliance.

The relationship to the process and the collaborators is ultimately what determines when and how to ask a question again. Attentiveness to the flow and style of show and artists will help to shape the dramaturg's questions and will offer a guide to how and when these questions will be most effective. The dramaturg has an idea of what she wants to accomplish through the asking or answering of a question, and including timing into the mindset will help to make that happen.

When to Offer Content

The timing of what to offer and when is a continuously evolving prospect for the dramaturg. He wants to provide the necessary information to help the rest of the production team develop the various elements of production. However, as mentioned earlier, too much too soon can be overwhelming and bringing in content too late makes it generally unusable.

One of the major contributions of the dramaturg in production is the output of information that helps provide context for the artistic collaboration. This takes many forms, which will be addressed in Chapter 7, though the form is important to consider in relation to the mindset of the dramaturg, particularly as it relates to the timing. The close attention paid in order to determine when best to ask a question is also needed when determining when to offer content to the artistic collaborators.

The most useful approach to content is to answer the question, "What is its purpose and who is it for?" It is a question and a point of view that is vital to effective content creation of all kinds, and will limit the dramaturg's confusion and uncertainty around what to include and when to provide. This simple clarification will reveal the kind of information as well as its form and timing. The purpose points to both who is the audience and when in the process. For example, content that is intended to bolster advance ticket sales will be addressed to potential audiences and happen early in the production cycle.

The recipient of the content determines what it will be and in turn when it will be effective. We can frame three categories based on its recipient: content for actors, content for directors, and content for audience. Each area requires a unique approach and the form, content and timing need to be consciously selected to be their most useful. This goes back to the earlier discussion of understanding the composition of the parts into the whole and requires an understanding of the unique needs of each group, as well as knowing how the pieces fit together and when. The actor needs a character-name pronunciation key early in the process, while the list of prompts for the audience talkback will be one of the last things completed. These categories will be looked at in more detail in later chapters of this book when specific areas of content are discussed. However, they are worth considering when thinking about the mindset, as the question of timing is decisively linked to the question of content.

TIP: Try something.

Once again, attention to the process is of paramount importance. When the dramaturg knows what goes into the various steps, she can better gauge what kind of content will be useful at what point in the process. A collection of visual imagery that could spark ideas and conversation about the landscape of the production can be an effective contribution in pre-production meetings. That same source would not be welcome just before load-in when that kind of creative exploration has been replaced by the deadline-driven experience of finalizing builds. Similarly, actors need the kind of general information about the world of the play as they are getting to know characters and getting acquainted with the work. Information about pronunciation, dialects, and locations are things that are needed around the first read-through; which is not a time that the characteristic of a nuanced psychological condition would be well placed.

Understanding what kind of content will be most effective at each phase of the project is part of the mindset, and equally important is keen attention to the kind of content to provide. Close communication as well as presence in rehearsal and production meetings allows the dramaturg to have up-to-date knowledge of the work that is going into the production from the various departments. The contextual input the dramaturg offers is not to do the visual and textual research for the other collaborators, but to bring in additional material and commentary to add to the work. In order to do that effectively, the dramaturg needs to know what is being done, looked at, discussed, and created. She needs to know when a new direction is selected so her input stays in line with the other artists. She also needs to see if a production element starts to go off course from the rest of the collaboration.

The timing of content also incorporates that which we offer audiences. Our access to potential audiences can start well before the production through various kinds of outreach media, and carries through to what audience members see as they walk away from the production. The timing is in part determined by the purpose: is it to entice audiences to see the show, to provide important data, or to challenge an understanding? Again, what is the purpose of this content and for whom is it intended? When creating materials for the theatrical audience, we are attentive to where they are in terms of location and time. Is this something that is going to be a targeted marketing blurb or the text in the program? Are we preparing them for what they will see or inspiring response when they walk out the door? The dramaturg's mindset is steeped in this question and it informs all of the information that she shares. The question is vital in shaping the what and the when of the content – what do you want it to accomplish?

Timing is determined by the effect desired. What do you want to provoke in the audience? Is this an opportunity to connect to more than the limits of a single show and specific audience? Are there artistic, institutional, and/or community needs that can be addressed in that content shared between dramaturg and audience? If so, at what point in the interaction would this content be most effective?

The question of efficacy is the foundation of every aspect of the mindset to dramaturg. The close attention to the kind of content we contribute, and particularly the timing with which we offer that content is going to significantly affect the usefulness of our efforts. Consequently, the importance of timing cannot be overstated when it comes to the contextual input of the dramaturg.

When to Offer Commentary

The next timing question is one that can sometimes be fraught and relies heavily on the relationships established with collaborators – when to offer commentary? The timing of this one includes the same considerations of useful and effective as any other contribution the dramaturg offers; however, commentary has an additional challenge. The dramaturg must contend with the possibility of seeming to "give notes" which is typically problematic in dramaturgical collaboration. The purpose is not to offer solutions or tell artistic collaborators what should be done; the purpose is to bring attention to elements that require care, so the time and manner in which commentary is offered necessarily contends with the possibility of being perceived as "notes."

There is a difference between the questions the dramaturg asks, which were discussed in some detail in Chapter 2, and the commentary he offers. Both are intended to provoke thought from the collaborator; however, while the question is asked to incite an active response, commentary is offered to be informative. Commentary provides a perspective on the event of the performance and is particularly useful when it is framed as a description of what the dramaturg sees. Often the term is used to describe the sharing of an opinion, which is not how the dramaturg best utilizes it. The mindset to dramaturg is developed through the use of descriptive and responsive commentary on what the dramaturg sees. This commentary has a clear critical point of view and is shaped by the knowledge he brings of both text and process; however, it describes rather than suggests, and is an important part of the mindset.

It can seem that it is merely a semantic difference, or that the dramaturg tries to avoid the appearance of critique while that is what he ultimately does. However, the credibility of the dramaturgical process is predicated on this ability to offer insight and input without the bias of how he thinks it should be done, or an implication that he is trying to direct/design/manage the show for his collaborators. This goes beyond how something is phrased and is essential to the mindset. In various stages of the process, the dramaturg responds to what he is given and offers a commentary that is pertinent, useful, and will continue to prompt the other theatre artists to shape the vision of the play. Everything that determines the dramaturgical viewpoint is shaped by the desire to bring a project to an audience in a manner that is as authentic and meaningful as possible.

Commentary is not opinion, and it is not part of the mindset to offer opinion. The most useful commentary is responsive and offers collaborators a view of what is being seen or heard. By definition a commentary is a descriptive account of an event and that can be a useful tool for collaborators. On the other hand, opinion is an individual judgment that is less effective for the dramaturgical mindset and can leak into the process and potentially cause resistance in the listener. The value of the dramaturg's commentary is that it is grounded in knowledge and carefully crafted, and ultimately intended to help the collaborator come to an effective artistic choice. Commentary invites conversation and inspires ideas where opinion lessens the effectiveness of the role as it forfeits the open, broad-based, holistic point of view. In short, opinions are lazy and less effective dramaturgy.

Since dramaturgy is a way of seeing and a way of engaging with material, both of these aspects are necessary when determining the timing of offering commentary. The dramaturg needs to have a clear view of the material as well as a deliberate and specific approach to and purpose for it. When that clarity of sight and function are in place, she will know what she is answering and to what end and this information will reveal the most effective timing of that offer.

The approach to discerning when to offer commentary is similar to that of the timing of asking questions. Once again the dramaturg looks for when it can be heard and when it is pertinent, with the ultimate goal of being useful for the individual production element and the project as a whole. The first has one very straightforward timeframe – offer commentary when it is requested. There are times where a director, designer or some other artist will ask directly to look at a particular element. It may be, "Is this scene working?" or, "Does this composition create a feeling of emptiness?" The direct request for commentary is a straightforward exchange and as long as care is taken to present it in a way that reflects that particular relationship and so the commentary is useful, there is not much to figure out.

Commentary is not always requested directly, and the need to determine timing and form becomes very important in these cases. There may be an invitation to come and "take a look" at something without a specific need or request. In those cases, when it is possible to establish expectations ahead of time that is preferable because it can help to clarify the exchange. However, it is frequently the case that the commentary comes from the ongoing relationship and presence in the process, and in those cases it is particularly important to attend to the timing in order for the observations to be both heard and useful.

One impediment to being heard as a dramaturg is offering commentary that provides the answer to how something should be done. When the dramaturg is no longer offering insight on what she sees and instead becomes a source of changes to make, the primary function as collaborator with a broad, holistic viewpoint is compromised. The ability to offer an open and responsive commentary on the elements of production while maintaining a perspective on the piece as a whole is essential to the work of the dramaturg. Once the remarks are proscriptive rather than responsive, the dramaturg no longer holds that position.

There are two ways to avoid this snare – one of form and the other one of timing. The form our comments take shapes their reception. When the dramaturg shapes the commentary to what is seen and tells the artistic collaborators what the experience of the work looks and feels like, and tells it with clarity and precision, then this is a usable analysis. The dramaturg has a specialized perspective on the work and her ability to reflect what is there and comment on what she sees at various stages in the process can offer her collaborators incredible insight into the reception of the artistic choices made. Because the dramaturg knows what is intended and is focused on what is there, she holds a unique position for commentary. That position is not one that we want to lose by offering suggestions on how to do the job of someone else on the production team. It is not only inappropriate to offer opinions on choices made by collaborators, it can be damaging to the process.

Whatever the project and whoever the collaborator, the chief asset of the dramaturg is the broad-based viewpoint and that is one we want to protect. However, when advice is sought or a direct question looking for a solution is asked, that can present a difficulty. It is a good general rule for the dramaturg to answer the question asked; however, when she sees the whole as well as the parts, the dramaturg recognizes that offering a solution may offer a short-lived resolution that results in a less effective collaboration long term. Questions are answered and commentary provided within the context of an established relationship. However, if it is at all possible to deflect the direct request for a solution into a conversation that helps to prompt ideas for that solution, that is generally more advantageous to the collaboration. One way to redirect the request for a solution is to offer commentary even when opinion is solicited. In other words, rather than offer an opinion on whether it makes sense for the character to exit through the audience, the dramaturg can describe the effect of her going through the audience and also the effect of her staying on the stage.

Timing is the other tool with which to approach the danger of becoming proscriptive in commentary. When it is provided gives more to the likelihood of commentary being heard and being useful than any other single element. Timing is also how a dramaturg can potentially avoid the complication of the direct question for a solution, if he can offer the solution at a time that gives the collaborator the prompt to think about it rather than an answer to attempt. That kind of resolution can often be straightforward; for example, something as simple as offering the suggestion at the end of the rehearsal rather than at the beginning will necessitate its being considered rather than immediately attempted. It really is a matter of attention, recognizing the value of a responsive commentary and staying closely attuned to when that is most usefully presented.

Once the comments are heard, the dramaturg wants to ensure they are useful, which is also a question of timing. As with the questions, the understanding of the process flow of the production and individual artists will help to determine this facet. Talking about broad-scale conceptual choices late in the production calendar when fine-tuning should be happening will not assist the process and will likely cause conflict since that level of artistic choice is not malleable at that stage. Consequently, those ideas are not heard and the credibility of the contribution is called into question. The reflection of what we see needs to be pertinent to the creation of the piece as a whole. There is a reason the dramaturg participates in the meeting or the rehearsal and there is a purpose to the questions, content, and commentary provided. If the input is not feeding into the creative process of the project then it is not effective dramaturgy.

What to Ask if It Has to Be Now

The dramaturg chooses the mode of communication that is best suited to the project and the timing that will most likely allow his work to be heard and pertinent. However, there are circumstances that preclude being able to choose the time to ask questions or provide input. There are a number of circumstances that may affect the timetable and remove the choice of timing from the dramaturg. It can be the production schedule, travel schedules, artist demands or any series of conditions that dictate when the dramaturgical contributions can be made.

The primary consideration is still one of efficacy, and if the dramaturg is unable to choose the "when," she can work within the given parameters and select the input that is most useful to the project. That will mean both prioritizing the content and looking critically at the timetable in order to see what aspects of content and questions will be pertinent within the given constraints. There may be content that would have been useful to design staff but which becomes less so at the point in the production schedule when she is able to offer it, and so she selects context that is useful to the project as a whole.

The process relies on the knowledge of the project in its pieces and its whole, and is the reverse of starting with content to determine timing. When the timing is specified, the dramaturg looks at where her work will be most effective, what can be heard and be pertinent in the time given. Whether this is one week of residence in the middle of the production calendar, or an hour a week with the director, or working completely with remote access and the time constraints that implies, the scope and scale of the response must be appropriate to the circumstances.

Timing will also affect the manner of how the content is shared. The various options of question, content, and commentary are usually dependent on the subject and collaborators. There are some kinds of conversations that are more easily sparked by questions and other kinds of work that is better served by sharing content. However, when the time is no longer flexible, the form will be driven as much by schedule as content. Even if the preferable mode for working with the director on the metaphor of the piece would be asking questions and creative brainstorming, if the time is limited and only at the very beginning of the process, a dramaturg may choose to provide content that illuminates certain kinds of metaphor to give concrete examples to add to the discussion.

When the timing is set in the production schedule, as with audience talkbacks or student matinees, the dramaturg finds the most important and useful points of contact within that context. If the goal is to inspire a student audience to learn more about the social issues attached to the play, the dramaturg will use the hour of post-show discussion to tailor the conversation to that end. Her study guide and any other content available will work with that goal in mind. The mindset is formed through close attention to timing, and the effective use of the time that is available. The dramaturg looks for ways to connect to the audience and act as the advocate for those who will be in the seats, and she will use her understanding of the order and schedule of events to ensure that advocacy is well established. If there are things the audience needs to know or ways to shape the entry into the world of the play, the mindset to dramaturg relies on the close attention to the process in order to use the time most productively.

Staying in the Moment

The dramaturg is an advocate for the eventual audience to the production and his work always includes some aspect of looking forward to that point in time. In addition, much of the context research that he does is often historical or even in a modern piece will be looking at the recent history of the writing of the play. Consequently, the idea of dramaturgy as being focused on the future is an unsurprising misunderstanding. However, a fundamental part of timing and essential to the dramaturgical mindset is to stay in the moment at all times. The dramaturg needs to be able to respond to what happens at the precise time and place in which something occurs. While there is an eye to what the audience will ultimately experience, the dramaturgical process moves through the production schedule in such a way that he offers input based on the particular moment.

The questions and comments the dramaturg makes in week two are specific to that point in the production and reflect the understanding of the process and the relationships forged with the artistic collaborators. To work effectively, he needs to reside completely in week two and connect clearly to the needs and demands of that particular point in the project. While the image of the whole production and where the collaborators hope to take it is part of his viewpoint, in order to offer substantial commentary, he needs to see the elements of production clearly in time, as well.

Staying in the moment helps to connect to the process as well as aiding the flexible thinking that is so important in dramaturgy. It requires attentiveness to change and a close watch on the progress of each production element in order to track the movement of the piece as a whole. It is precisely the kind of attentiveness that the dramaturgical mindset inspires. When the dramaturg looks clearly at what is presented, taken on its own terms and seen in specific time as part of the composition of a whole, that is the frame of reference from which he can dramaturg.

Dramaturgy is a way to see, and a significant facet of that vision is shaped by time. Understanding how the production timeline affects how and what we ask or provide to the collaborators allows us to be more effective in the artistic process. Each element of the project has its own purpose and timeline, and the dramaturg can work at the intersection of those elements and move through time with them. Consequently, when she offers commentary on what she sees, it is seen in its moment. This continues to be important through the process as the ultimate presence of the audience will be the final case of seeing only what is presented in the present moment in time. As much as the dramaturg can create a resemblance to that experience, the more information the artistic collaboration will have and the more effective the dramaturgy will be.

The "Elephant in the Room"

The metaphor of the elephant in the room refers to the obvious issue that is being ignored, and it has also come to include a problem or concern that people refuse to address. It is a wonderful image, and one that has particular resonance for theatre artists. It is our job to talk about the things that are important, and difficult, and sometimes exactly the things that people want to pretend are not there. Part of the power of this metaphor is that it is not something hidden or obscured; it is a big, giant presence that is being willfully ignored.

There is something to the image of the giant elephant in the middle of the room, perhaps most delightfully explored by the English artist Banksy in the 2006 Los Angeles show "Barely Legal." Banksy is a subversive and secretive graffiti artist, filmmaker and activist. His work in the streets and the galleries and showings around the world has an artistry that shows the combination of provocative, thoughtful, and prankster that characterizes the work. The LA warehouse exhibit was based on the theme of global poverty, and the centerpiece was an 8,000 pound live elephant painted red with gold fleurs-de-lis in the middle of an elegant room.

The topic is so conspicuous that it cannot be missed while at the same time attention to it is deliberately and markedly avoided. It is an apt analogy and a practice that runs counter to the work of the dramaturg. His purpose is to see the whole and the parts and offer input and commentary in time to help move the project closer to the audience experience being sought. In order to do that, he necessarily and actively sees what is presented and what is implied. While there is always the possibility of missing something, willful avoidance is something that is directly in opposition to his role in the production. The deliberate and willful revelations of the elements that are avoided are more in line with dramaturgy.

The ignored issue may be a difficult element inherent in the project or something that is done by an artistic collaborator, and it is the responsibility of the dramaturg to determine where and when the input needs to be placed. Typically it will be first addressed with the collaborating artists and whatever resolution can be reached will happen within the production team. However, if there is not agreement about the nature of, or even presence of the metaphoric elephant, the dramaturg may need to address it with the audience.

We can look at this as two separate elephants, the one in the room with the production team and the one in the room with the audience. They are each conspicuous, important, and potentially fraught and they require differing approaches.

The dramaturg is the surrogate for the audience throughout the production process as a point of reference for the production team. She can articulate an audience point of view for the various members of the company throughout the process.

The idea of the view of the audience has come up a few times, and it is worth noting there is no monolithic viewpoint of "audience." The theatrical audience is a collection of individuals and is different each performance, each place. One of the primary dynamic elements of live performance is the presence of an audience and the differing perspectives that introduces. The thing that unites the group of individuals is the shared experience of the performance; they are sharing time and place in a way that creates a kind of community for that period of time. When the audience is referenced, it is with that in mind, the collection of people who gather for the event of the performance. The different perspectives and responses to the work are taken into account, and often are particularly useful for the dramaturg.

The dramaturg is the advocate for the audience in relation to the artistic collaborators to help them connect the elements of production into a cohesive whole for the eventual audience. Again he is looking for the coherent read of the production while recognizing different points of view among the audience. The dramaturg helps prepare the production staff and the audience for the experience of seeing the show through the distribution of content, questions and commentary for those behind and in front of the stage. He sometimes acts as spokesperson for the audience, asking the questions or helping to frame the conversations that the project will inspire.

There are times when the conversation needs to be framed because it is a difficult one, and this requires particular attention from the dramaturg. It can arise from a problematic element in the play or the production, such as a controversial notion or theme. It may stem from some disagreement during the artistic process about what needs to be addressed, possibly due to conflict within the company about the implication of an action. For example, there was a new play with a sexual scene between a student and her teacher that caused some conflict within the production team. The playwright intended the scene to be viewed as rape; however, the director did not feel the text supported that read and saw the scene more about challenging the idea of consent within a power dynamic. The cast was also somewhat split on the action of the scene and it caused conflict in rehearsal in addition to making the scene less specific and ultimately less effective. While the dramaturg does not undermine the work of the rest of the artistic team, there are times when she needs to address questions and concerns by drawing attention to "the elephant in the room."

The Company Elephant

The very idea of the elephant in the room is touchy. It implies there is something that cannot be missed and is willfully ignored by those present. Consequently, one of the things the dramaturg should attend to when approaching these kinds of issues is the reason why they are being ignored. Once she has a sense of why it is overlooked, she can better navigate through in order to reveal it in a useful manner. The idea of useful permeates this aspect of dramaturgy, as well. The choice to point out what is being ignored is made with a purpose in mind. If it is not necessary, if it is not important, there is no value in pointing to the elephant; however, when it is something that affects the company or the narrative, it needs to be brought to light.

The situation with the contested rape scene mentioned earlier is an example of a rehearsal elephant that needs to be addressed. The notion of consent and the presentation of sexual abuse are themselves issues that incite reaction, and to ignore the conflict around the reading of the scene will not add to the strength of the piece or the relations among the company. Ultimately the scene is going to be played how the director directs it, and the dramaturg cannot undermine that artistic choice. What he can do is facilitate a conversation between the director and playwright regarding the scene to see if there is a common purpose to be found. For the cast, he can bring in materials about power dynamics in sexuality, sexual harassment, college assault, legal definitions and stories. In short, as much as possible, the dramaturg can prompt the conversation about the issues raised. These conversations will likely happen outside the rehearsal room. It is not a subversion of the process of staging the show, but can be an addition to the materials the company shares. Ideally this will help shape the scene into a clear and decisive narrative, while at the same time it is helping the company address the issues it confronts.

The elephant in the rehearsal room can be related to content, process, or personality, and part of the holistic view of the dramaturg is to see how all of the pieces are coming together. It is not simple to read the situation, nor an easy process to introduce those potentially contentious issues. However, part of the role is to help the company see the elephants they need to see in order to tell the story to the audience.

The ability to see the elephant in the room for the company is important; however, it is even more within the mandate of the dramaturgical mindset to see the elephant in the room with the audience. The issues and choices that a production introduces to an audience can cause a kind of conflict or unrest that may necessitate additional dramaturgical input.

The Audience and the Elephant

The dramaturg can give an audience room and language to respond to challenging aspects of the performance. She can provide the forum of a talkback or can use the access point of program notes and lobby display or other forms of direct audience outreach. One challenge when addressing the elephant in the room is making certain that it is in fact in the room, and not merely a personal response. For example, the dramaturg sees a real problem with cultural appropriation in the production. The questions and commentary she offers the director are dismissed and become borderline contentious. The dramaturg continues to work the show, offering the input she can and preparing a context within which to address cultural appropriation with the audience, if the need arises. She does not seek a "gotcha" moment for the director, nor try to undermine the goals of the production. Instead she recognizes the likelihood that the audience will see what she did and will welcome an opportunity to address the questions raised.

The training and habit of being responsive is of great assistance, and the dramaturg needs to take her cue from the audience even after setting up the place for the difficult conversation. The context is there in the audience outreach; however, not as input to create the reaction but as a frame through which to respond to it. If the audience is not concerned about the "elephant" issue, it may not need the spotlight. Once again, the attentive, responsive and in-the-moment dramaturg will be able to support the audience experience in a way that frames the conversations that need to happen. The balance between recognizing the elephant created by a production choice and not undermining or sabotaging that choice can be a challenge that requires the open, flexible thinking of the mindset. For example, if a director makes a casting choice that is controversial – perhaps a racial or ethnic change that may be provocative – the elephant is the choice, not the effect of that choice for an individual audience member. The framing of the talkback or the program note then can be racial or ethnic representation on stage as a way to recognize the element that everyone in the room sees but is typically asked to ignore, and an environment can be created where the audience can further explore the implications of what they saw.

Pointing out the elephant requires the same level of care and attention as any other element of dramaturgy. It demands understanding of process as well as timing, and has to have a specific reason to be done. The purpose can coincide with production needs or with audience outreach, and the dramaturg needs a clear view on what purpose is being served in order to shape the form and timing of her revelation. There may be times when the issue merely needs to be acknowledged as an omission – we as a production are choosing to avoid that specific topic in favor of this other one. This is the kind of input that can be done directly, highlighted in a program note or in the production's marketing materials. The attention paid to the ignored element, shining the light on the elephant, can have any number of results, be it the sharing of information or the commiserating of an opportunity missed. Regardless of the outcome, the dramaturg tries to honestly approach the issues raised by a play and through a production. She seeks to consider and explore these issues in ways that shape a meaningful experience for the audience.

The dramaturg does not have the luxury to ignore the elephant in the room, and the need to illuminate it is integral to the mindset. The dramaturg gives context, responds to what is presented and sees with an eye that is both on the entire project and focused on the current moment. Those attributes do not coexist with the willful disregard of a concern or the hope that something will go unnoticed by the future audience. The attentive and responsive perspective is one that exists based on its ability to see clearly, think flexibly, and respond usefully. The dramaturg shines the light on the elephant in the room for all of his audiences.

Timing is absolutely vital to the mindset to dramaturg. Understanding when a contribution is necessary makes the work effective, and the usefulness of that contribution depends on the close attention to the process. Productions and projects have a schedule and an agenda, and the better the dramaturg understands that movement, the more closely she will be able to fit into that process. Timing will shape what and how she contributes and is the most direct way to gain the viewpoint from which to see clearly and offer useful input. This attention to timing joins with the ability to see holistically and to use questions effectively in order to develop a dramaturgical mindset – a way to see and engage with material.

Summary

The mindset to dramaturg is established through close attention to timing. Understanding how to incorporate the dramaturgical input into the production schedule as well as recognizing when that input will be most useful are both important skills to develop as a dramaturg.

5

WHY THIS, HERE, NOW?

> *The dramaturg facilitates a series of pre- and post-show discussions organized around the principle of justice. She invites community activists, clergy, legal experts, and former convicts for a whole program organized around the idea of crime and punishment, ethical and legal considerations, community concerns and rehabilitation. The play she is dramaturging is a piece about the interrogation tactics of a totalitarian regime. It is brutal, disturbing, and in many ways far removed from the regional theatre audience she anticipates. A well-established repertory theatre company in a major city in the Northeastern United States is producing the play. The theatre has a strong subscriber base as well as a large student and young professional audience. There has been a shooting in the community within the past year and the public discussions are still heated around issues such as gun control and police control. The dramaturg uses the idea of crime and punishment in the community context as a way to bring this audience into the world of the play and offer some context that will help it seem less remote to this audience in that place.*

It is the fundamental question of theatre-making and should be part of all aspects of the selection and production process: Why this play, for this audience, at this moment?

There are so many ways the question of why this play is answered just in the selection process. The mission statement of a company is going to play a part, as is its casting pool, its audience, its physical location, the availability of rights, the technical requirements, the rest of the season, and the seasons before. The practicality of why the play is selected and the artistic choices that support the production's "here" and "now" have tangible as well as artistic considerations. A season is selected for a given time and place and is also made with close attention to the various ways a play can speak to an audience. A director chooses her concept and a designer's work is based on the point of communication to the audience. Not a generic or hypothetical audience, but the one drawn from the members of that community from that time and place. Actors present directly to that particular community and all of the publicity, outreach, educational, and development materials are customized to the specificity of a group in a place and a time.

This three-part question – why this, here now? – provides the foundation of the mindset to dramaturg and it is these topics that tie together the elements. This chapter examines each part as a separate question, while acknowledging they are intertwined and interdependent and it is their combination that creates a fundamental aspect of the mindset to dramaturg. The tactics of asking and answering questions, the holistic viewpoint and attention to timing work together in order to make the production as closely attuned to the three questions as possible. Each selection made, each question asked, every play chosen and every piece of audience outreach is predicated on these questions. The choices are deliberate and specific and geared to an event in a particular place at a particular time for a particular audience.

Why this, here, now? Each part of the question has its own process of discovery. All of the contributions and tasks the dramaturg performs with and for the production team and audience ultimately reflect the attentiveness to these vital parameters. The research and input the dramaturg offers is not generalized for productions of the play. Sometimes the question arises: why not use the dramaturgy from a previous production? However, the work that is general enough to be transferable is not going to be particularly effective. The mindset and output is tailored to the specific production the dramaturg is working on, and that production has a particular audience and a specific time. The pieces of the mindset dovetail into the specificity of this play, here and now, and that knowledge characterizes the input and the output the dramaturg provides throughout the production process.

Why This Play?

The first parameter is the play – why this play? This element is addressed early in the process if the dramaturg is involved in the season planning. When that is the case, the issues that are raised include both the practical and philosophical. Some of the practical considerations include the nature of the producing theatre, such as if there is a resident company with casting requirements. There are questions of resources in terms of time, personnel, and budget. Theatre space and configuration will play a part, as well as the kind of work offered by the theatre community in the area. Play selection will also take into consideration the kinds of work offered in previous seasons, influence of a subscriber base, desire of the resident artists, and time of year.

There are a host of practical considerations that are part of season planning. The dramaturgical input can assist that process as well as the more philosophical or artistic considerations of play selection. These philosophical considerations generally consist of the mission statement of the theatre, the overall theme or purpose of the season, as well as the conversations and interactions to have with the audience. The selection of a particular play is determined by the understanding of who the audience is, what they want to and/or should talk about. Are there specific social or political issues that are of particular significance in the community? Have there been incidents or events that have gotten attention on a community scale? What kind of questions and ideas will challenge them? Inspire them? What do we need to be talking about? Play selection is an opportunity to find work that will be meaningful and significant for the audience. It will reflect the kind of art the company wants to create and the audiences for whom it is created.

It is useful to ask the question throughout the process. Why this play? It is not a question asked only during play selection, and often the dramaturg will not be a part of the season planning so he examines this question for the first time when he begins working on the production. Why this play? Wherever he first encounters the play, in selection or in production, the answer needs to be found in order to enhance the experience for the audience.

When the dramaturg is involved in play selection he is privy to the conversations around the practical and philosophical considerations behind the choice and those conversations will help frame the dramaturgical framework of why this play. If he is not part of the selection, he starts with the script and initial conversations with collaborators to get some sense of what came before, though ultimately it is a matter of text and production that illuminates the answer to that question. Why this play is a dramaturgical question and is answered through a broad-based point of view on the meaning and import of the story being told.

Why this play? For example, a theatre company chooses a season of work dedicated to contemporary American women playwrights. The artistic management decided to take an active part in the national discussion around gender parity in the theatre by producing a season of women writers. They select *Intimate Apparel* by Lynn Nottage, *The Flick* by Annie Baker, *The Language Archive* by Julia Cho, *Eurydice* by Sarah Ruhl, and *Topdog/Underdog* by Suzan-Lori Parks. It is a collection of award-winning plays with a range of styles and subjects that will provide a theatrically diverse season. The goal is to produce more plays by women playwrights and to inspire conversations about gender parity in the theatre.

Why this play? Looking at another example, a university program is dedicated to producing classics. The program director selects Shakespeare's *Antony and Cleopatra* and John Dryden's 1677 telling of the same story *All for Love*. This selection allows for an exploration of language and story point of view, as well as examining somewhat lesser-known classics from the period.

We do theatre because it matters, and we hope to never squander an audience. The play is not performed because it mattered to another audience; it is done because it has something to say to our audience. So the mindset of the dramaturg is shaped through the close attention to all the points of contact he can bolster between the play and the performance, between the production and its audience.

TIP: Be yourself and trust your own responses.

The first read of a script begins the process of exploration for the answer to the question why this play. The dramaturg acquaints herself with story, character and the world of the play and in doing so looks for the aspects of the piece that create the broader narrative, that offer the potential points of connection and conversation. She makes note of the social, political, philosophical questions that are asked by the play. She looks at the given circumstances of the play, not only to understand the mechanics of how to put it into production, but to evaluate what these circumstances imply and what they may offer to the discourse.

Why this play? A company is doing a production of Arthur Miller's *Death of a Salesman* and the production finds resonance with a young audience who can connect quite directly to the conflict between the life that is expected of you and the life you want to live.

Throughout the production process the dramaturg compiles the narrative for "Why this play?" It is a way to help connect the elements of the production into a cohesive whole and help the collaborating artists maintain the connection. "Why this play?" is the question that prompts the ability and the need to look at the piece holistically and be seeing it as a composite whole even while the pieces are being assembled. It often becomes the basis for the audience outreach materials that we generate.

TIP: Listen.

The question is straightforward; however, it rarely has a simple answer. The complexity of the work of a playwright and a production necessarily make it a more nuanced exchange, which is one of the reasons it is ongoing throughout the production. The answer takes into consideration what is known about the intent of the writer as well as the objective of the production. What we are trying to say is intrinsically linked to why this play and so the production concept or vision will necessarily be connected to the conversation. The dramaturg takes that further and looks at how that message is constructed as part of the evidence she gathers to answer. However, it is perhaps better to phrase it as a conversation rather than an answer, even though the idea is presented as a question. It is not a simple call and response and typically does not lend itself to a single, narrow answer. While we need to find specific and concrete elements to connect, they are a composite not a single response. The "why this play" is a prompt for the conversation that happens between the production and the audience.

Why Here?

Here points to multiple levels of space, including the performance space, the specific location, in what city or town, and what part of that place, and the larger location. A play performed at the American Repertory Theater is happening at the Loeb Drama Center, at Harvard University, in Cambridge, Massachusetts, across the river from Boston, in New England, in the Northeast, in the United States, as part of what we designate as the Western theatre. In addition, here is also whom – it is the audience for whom the play is performed. Any of those "here" have resonance and can provide an entry point for the dramaturgical work.

Plays are not presented to a live audience because they mattered to someone else. Artists produce plays because they believe the play has something to say to their audiences. Whether they were written five hundred years ago or are being devised for the production, the focus is on the specific presentation to a particular audience. It is the audience that characterizes a large portion of the "here" in the equation. The space that is occupied is space shared, so the "here" of the production necessarily includes the people who gather to see it. The audience is the recipient of the production and is the accomplice to the discussion it inspires. In determining "Why here?" it is as much the group who gathers as it is the place they assemble.

The play does not need to be about us to be meaningful to us, which is important to remember when making the connections between play and audience. There is no need to try to force a direct point of contact that is explicit to the world of the audience, no need to try to make it about these people and their world. Why here is found through resonance. What are the ideas, characters, notions that speak to the audience? What makes the play worth presenting to this audience, and what is necessary that they see?

The pieces the dramaturg finds in the text and what she compiles from the ideas of the collaborating artists are assessed and assembled based on the anticipated audience, and what she comes up with as the point of discussion for why this play is shaped for that conversation with the audience to answer the question why here. Once again, it is a series of questions that bring about the combined answer. What is happening in the area? What kinds of issues and circumstances are parts of the community dialogue? Which ones are being ignored?

The dramaturg understands the need to connect directly to the audience to inspire the conversations around this important question. Consequently, she strives to know who they are and the kinds of things they contend with. Of course the audience is large and diverse, we hope, so we look for broad ideas and issues and do not seek a standardized perspective or experience. We look for the things that will speak to members of the audience in a meaningful way in order to connect more directly with them throughout the production and its outreach.

Why here? A theatre company selects Anna Deavere Smith's play *Twilight: Los Angeles 1992*. The theatre has a racially diverse audience and is located in a city that has recently seen protests and violence around police treatment of suspects. Smith's one-person show is a series of monologues that were created from interviews with people who were directly and indirectly involved in the Los Angeles riots following the acquittal of the police officers charged with assaulting Rodney King. The play is intended to connect the historical event to the current climate in a way that allows the audience to confront the issues being faced by the community.

Here also refers to location and the place in which the theatrical event happens is an important consideration. This covers the performance space, neighborhood, region, and nation. Starting with space, the relative intimacy or vastness of the performance space is going to shape the nature of the visual landscape created by the collaborators as well as the experience of seeing it. If the performance happens in a non-traditional space, as some kind of installation, outside, or on any interior stage configuration, there is a difference in how the material is received and the spectators' relationship to the events onstage. The dramaturg is attentive to that aspect as well, and helps to guide the experience onstage and off to make the discussion as relevant as possible in that specific space.

Why here? A group wants to explore the language and style of medieval theatre and presents *The Second Shepherds' Play* from the Wakefield Cycle. The company produces the play in a large, open field. The production highlights the pastoral theme and emphasizes the lonely expanse of the characters' solitude by moving the audience through a comparable kind of landscape.

Generally in most city settings the concept of place includes the city block and the continent on which the performance happens, where the theatre physically resides, and we make note of the elements of place that can be used to connect to our audience. The audience moves through the external location to get to the performance, so the concept of "here" widens to include the events that happen in the area, and also the condition of the place itself. The topography, the relative upkeep, the view can all be an influential element to the audience experience. The classical Greek amphitheatres were constructed in such a way that the backdrop to the plays was the Greek world. It was vast and impressive and placed the tragedies in the context of a larger world and placed the audience at a vantage point to experience the stories from that perspective. The theatres that operate in precarious locations, that carry with them a feeling of danger, or one of consumerism and complacence, all affect the experience of the play. And all are part of the dramaturg's attention and make up her response to "Why here?"

TIP: See as much performance as you can.

Location is an incredibly powerful element and is one that needs to be an operating principle in the dramaturgical mindset. While the world of the play is firmly established, through the various means that create it, it is a place that is superimposed onto a real place, created in a space that has a simultaneous identity of a conventional space. Rather than try to pretend the world of the play erases the multiple levels of place, we try to figure out ways to use them to enhance the experience of the performance. The performance is happening in a real place, and that place is integral to the understanding of it. When we connect to the who and the where, we can bring the production to a more meaningful connection and more relevant conversation. What is happening where we perform? What does it look like? What does it sound like? What are the things that make it unique? What about this place is going to connect the audience more completely to the place we are creating for them?

Why here? The answer is connected to the place and may vary greatly even within the same work. One company may select the play because of the geographical connection to the playwright while another may select the same play for a circumstantial connection to the story. Why here tells us one of the ways the audience is specifically engaged with the piece.

The challenge for the dramaturg is to navigate the multiple levels of place and person in order to keep in mind why this play is happening for this audience. And ultimately make that as consequential an experience as possible. The dramaturg shapes the findings and makes the discussion inspired by "Why this play?" into a discussion with this specific audience in a particular place and by doing so establish "Why here?"

Why Now?

The final part of the equation is temporal, and this is perhaps the most exciting element of theatrical performance. It happens now, in time.

With contemporary technology there are so many forms of media in which a person has the capacity to work outside time, recorded with playback capability in the time and pace that the audience may prefer. A live performance exists in real time, and can be experienced only in that manner. Consequently, when talking about theatre, time becomes an important component and one that is necessary for the dramaturg to consider. The time of the performance, the experience of a real-time event, and most importantly the time during which these things occur.

Why this play now? In the same way that artists do not perform because it was important to some other audience, they do not select a play because it was relevant at some other time. Plays are done to say something to the given audiences at this moment in time. The experience of the production will be shaped to some degree by the circumstances of the time in which it is produced, and the more attentive the production is to this fact the better. Large and small issues affect the world of the audience which in turn affects the experience as an audience member. Theatre companies that operate during wartimes, where plays are performed during outbreaks of violence, are marked by that reality.

Time of day and time of year will affect the experience; however, the "Why now?" really addresses the larger influences of time that are felt by a community. A play exists in its own time, yet it happens in our time. As dramaturgs we look to link those things in such a manner that they inform each other. How can this play offer insight into the time in which we live? How does our experience in the world shape our understanding of the play? How can the play reveal something about the time in which we live? Once again, the purpose is not to make the play about now, but to find the points of contact to now; to recognize the power of the temporal reality of the theatre, coexisting in the time of the play and the time of the audience.

Why this play now? Arthur Miller played directly with temporal layers when he wrote *The Crucible*. He used the Salem witch trials as an analogy for the contemporary politics of Joseph McCarthy and the House Un-American Activities Committee. He wrote the play with the idea of existing in both worlds, offering the late seventeenth century as a way to speak directly to the politics of the1950s. Audiences now read and see it with a twenty-first-century point of view and when the play is performed now, it contends with the three times in a way that can offer a tremendous dramaturgical potential.

Another kind of time experienced in production is the theatrical moment. While the play is happening for the audience at the time in which they experience it, it is also part of a larger scope of performance and will be affected by the conventions, practices, and tenets of that moment. The play is shaped by all of these aspects: the time of the audience, the time of the play, and when it exists in the performance tradition itself. All of these aspects will affect the experience of the audience and so all must be part of the consideration of the dramaturg in order to augment the connection of audience to production.

Why now? Sometimes the play is going to reflect the things that are happening to the audience and sometimes the play will consciously reject them. It can ask important questions or introduce notions that are pertinent to the moment in which it is seen. And it can allow for an escape from the time and place of the audience reality. Regardless of what is sought, the dramaturg is conscientious about the time and one of her primary responsibilities throughout the production timeline is the compilation of material for the discussion prompted by the challenge: why this, here, now? The audience at a live performance experiences the event of the performance. While they are privy to the action of the play, spectators to that time and place, the event itself happens in actual time and space and creates a dynamic event. That is the point of connection and the resonance of the performance. It is the fact that something happens in the presentation of story in real time. Our job as theatre artists is to help ensure that something is meaningful.

The production team creates the world of the play. They offer the audience a visual and aural landscape to show a time and place in which to encounter a story. However, outside the real or conceptual door of that story is a time and place in which the audience lives. The point of true connection between audience and play is formed by the overlaps of those times and places. Not necessarily in an explicit sense, but in the conceptual ways in which the play reveals for the spectator something about her world, and how her world can offer insight into the play. It is the conversation that happens around the story told. It is the conversation that reveals why this play for this audience in this place at this time.

Again: Why This Play, Here, Now?

The dramaturg answers this three-part question from the first read of the script through the final post-show discussion. It is what shapes the work with the production team and is the point of reference for his role as advocate for the audience. The dramaturg's mindset is steeped in the relevance of the work, in the reason it needs to be seen by its audience. This chapter has looked primarily at the way a production dramaturg with a set script will answer the question in relationship to the audience. However, the dramaturg also offers the context for this discussion with the artistic collaborators and audience of any project. His questions asked and answered, his input, and the content he provides are all in support of clearly asserting why this play, here and now.

The dramaturgical mindset is reliant on flexible and creative thinking. It demands close attention to detail while staying open to a "big picture" point of view. It asks us as dramaturgs to be conspicuously present in the moment while maintaining an awareness of the point in the future in which we meet the audience. It requires constant vigilance toward the time, place, and relevance of the performance and pushes us to understand more about the time and place in which we create. Our understanding of the play needs to extend beyond the mechanics of the script and the demands of the elements of production and incorporate a nuanced comprehension of the meaning and consequence of the play. We are charged with intimate understanding of both the where of the play and the where of the production. Finally, we are given the task of navigating the time of the play as well as the time in which it occurs.

A theatrical performance should matter, and the way in which that is best understood is through the continued exploration of the important proposition – this play, here, now – that is an essential aspect of the mindset to dramaturg.

Summary

The mindset to dramaturg is based on the idea that the most important question to ask is, "Why?" The work of the dramaturg is focused on strengthening the points of connection to time, place, and audience.

Part II

SKILLSET

6

DRAMATURG AS PRACTICE

Using the word "dramaturg" as a verb is a way to define how the dramaturg should approach a project. It also is a way to define how a dramaturg should execute that project. As an action word, the verb "to dramaturg" starts with a mindset that allows us to be more useful in our collaborations and more effective with our contribution. It is a way to listen, question, excavate, connect, explore, bridge, advocate, support, synthesize, articulate, advise, curate, and contextualize. To dramaturg is to do, and the perspective is vital, because it is what allows for the practice, without limiting the scope to merely the application of a methodology.

The advantage a mindset has over a process is that it is flexible. When dramaturgy is considered as a way of seeing, a manner of engagement – when dramaturg is seen as a verb – it allows for a dynamic relationship to material rather than an exercise of applied process. The mindset to dramaturg is to be actively engaged in a project, with a holistic perspective, a responsive point of view, and a collaborative practice. The first part of this book looked at ways to develop this mindset, this way of seeing, and considered the role of dramaturg through a different lens. Part II looks at the application of the mindset, and how it can be applied to projects.

The mindset to dramaturg is developed in order to be a more effective artistic collaborator, and once it is understood as a way of seeing and engaging, it can then be used to effectively fulfill the necessary tasks of production, new play, or institutional dramaturgy; or really any kind of project to undertake. A person can curate an experience for an audience in many ways, and as long as she recognizes the audience and understands the experience, she can dramaturg.

The disadvantage of the flexible and adaptable nature of dramaturgy is that it seems to cover so many possibilities that it becomes difficult to identify the concrete of it. If it can be so many things, does that mean it is nothing in particular? Is there something about the open-ended and flexible nature of the dramaturgical perspective – the read of dramaturg as verb – that makes it so encompassing as to offer no specific guideline to the work we hope to do? Is it merely another way to arrive at the same impasse that sometimes seems to plague the field, "What is dramaturgy?"

Practicing dramaturg as verb allows for the ambiguity to be an asset and is itself a way to shape the method of dramaturgy. Since it is a way to see, it can be applied to any project. Since it is a way to process information, it can be useful to many different circumstances. Since it is a way to actively respond, it can be an asset to any collaboration. It halts the inclination to box dramaturgy into a simple process and recognizes it is both a way of seeing and a way of doing.

Asking questions, flexible thinking, seeing holistically, understanding timing, and a close connection to the needs of the audience are all part of the dramaturgical mindset. To dramaturg is a way of looking at the world, a perspective that can be applied to every facet of life and one that is an asset for a theatre maker. However, while it is a mindset, it is important to remember that it is not only a mindset. To dramaturg is also a dynamic practice that incorporates the mindset. It is the way to use the outlook in order to shape the output on a project. It is a method that will help make the contribution to any project more effective.

The flexibility of dramaturgy ultimately means that the work of the dramaturg is defined by the needs of the project. The more closely he connects to those needs, the more useful the dramaturg's role. Each new venture is approached with openness and clarity in order to determine what is needed and for whom. These will in turn reveal how that input can best be offered. The concrete foundation of dramaturgy is not found in the specificity of the task or its requirements; however, it is best to identify a process that is applicable to the tasks of the dramaturg and incorporates the mindset to dramaturg.

The method of dramaturgy is formed by two fundamental questions that provide the context that informs every task: What is its purpose? Who is it for? The clarity and usefulness of the mindset and its application to method is shaped by the ability to stay clearly connected to these parameters – what and who – and each step and each task will be built on that foundation.

The Method

As introduced in the first chapter, the method to dramaturg has three steps and the overall success of the work is dependent on how effectively the three work in concert.

The three steps are simple: define the project, gather the content, and communicate the findings. It is a deceptively simple and straightforward process and can decidedly shape the way we work as dramaturgs in any context. While simple, it is not always easy to do these things well, and the craft of dramaturgy is in the honing of those skills. In addition, the real test of effectiveness is in the combination of the steps. Each is as important as the others, and if they are not all three useful collectively, the efficacy of the dramaturgy may be significantly reduced.

The usefulness in concert is something that is worth taking some time to discuss as it is another example of the whole being greater than the sum of the parts. It is not just that the three steps need to be well done, but they are interconnected in a way that creates the dynamic synthesis of the work – that creates a dramaturgical output. Metaphor is effective to discuss the dramaturgical process and we can use a construction one. The dynamic connection of the steps is akin to the composition of concrete. For example, people sometimes confuse the words and misuse concrete and cement as interchangeable terms; however, cement is a component of concrete. Cement is the sticky substance that combines with sand, gravel, stone, or other particles to bond and form usable concrete. It is the combination of the materials that results in a useful substance of concrete.

Perhaps a better metaphor is from chemistry; think about the process and product of dramaturgy as akin to the difference between a mixture and a compound. A mixture is a combination of elements while a compound has the elements react in such a way that something new is formed. And it is not a combination that can be separated by physical means once that dynamic joining has occurred. Or another metaphor that can be used is thinking of cooking ingredients that have a form and texture as separate elements but when combined form something completely different. The cooking analogy works well because when they are combined in an effective manner they can form something extraordinary.

There are many analogies and ways to look at the kind of connection that dramaturgical process demands. These offer some insight into the inextricable link between the attention paid to the process and the effectiveness of the product. The comparison also helps to remind one that the combination of the steps in the process is what brings about the dynamic yield – the composition of the recipe produces the cake. The ingredients must be in the effective measure and treatment in order to bring the desired result. The analogy reiterates that the effectiveness of the dramaturg's work relies on each of the steps in the process of creation in equal measure. It is their fusion that provides the output of the dramaturg and this output will ultimately be the primary contribution to the creative collaboration.

Step 1: Define the Project

As previously mentioned, the extensive practice explaining dramaturgy to those who ask what one does for a living is useful preparation to practice dramaturgy. The ability to understand what is asked and to answer coherently is a required skill for a dramaturg. In addition, the ability to work with and around ambiguity is an important part of the work. This ambiguity is often navigated through the construction of definitions – of words, ideas, and processes.

The mindset of the dramaturg is largely forged through definition. Defining is a process of making something clear or distinct and this is precisely the kind of involvement the dramaturg hopes to have in the creative process. It is not being a translator or an intermediary between script and actor or playwright and director, rather it is a process with the goal of clarity and specificity for whatever audience she is targeting.

The distinction between definition and translation is important in understanding the unique collaborative role of dramaturg. One of the things that causes confusion, and sometimes suspicion, in a production team is the image of translator that indicates that the dramaturg essentially stands between the collaborators, or between the material and artist, and is the point of comprehension between them. In short, the implication is that the work needs to be translated or reframed. Definition, on the other hand, is a way to strengthen connections, to broaden and deepen comprehension, not supplant it. The dramaturg does not stand as a barrier of translation between the source and target, but as an additional point of connection through definition. To use another metaphor, she serves as the current connecting collaborators, ideas, and materials.

The act of making something clear or distinct is a useful frame for looking at the tasks of the dramaturg, and as an action it encompasses the process. In short, the practice of defining permeates the dramaturg's work. The collaborative process itself requires a kind of clarifying and one of the first things we do with artists with whom we work is to discuss needs and expectations. This is somewhat built in to the first meetings with directors and playwrights where we talk about the various possibilities for the collaboration and try to ensure that the expectations of the role of dramaturgy in the process are mutually understood. The conversation should also happen with actors and other members of the production team and it is useful to set the tone of open communication and clarity of expectation early in the process.

The following are some examples of different ways to dramaturg on a production, depending on the needs of the company and definition of the project. They demonstrate the flexibility of the mindset and the way the collaboration can determine the efficacy of the role.

Example: Dramaturg as Collaborator

A first meeting with a director is a chance to get a sense of her ideas for the play, her communication style and why she is interested in a particular work. It is also an opportunity to get a sense of her expectations of dramaturgy in the production. This input will be valuable to help define the process of collaborating with the director.

A director likes to talk through the large thematic ideas of the play and the time period. She sees the dramaturg as a point of contact to explore the ideas of the play in a more informal, conversational way, and potentially test out ideas. She does not want materials from the dramaturg, nor does she want him to be actively involved in the rehearsal process. This kind of starting point is useful because the expectation is clearly articulated; however, it sets somewhat strict parameters. Later there is always the

(continued)

(continued)

possibility that the dramaturg will be able to find a more expansive role in the production; however, it is also useful to define the role in a way that will make it as effective as possible within the expectation.

The dramaturg has a standing meeting with the director before rehearsal. He does not bring in physical materials but comes to each meeting with a talking point related to the scene being worked that rehearsal. His contextual research around the ideas of the play and the cultural circumstances provide the foundation for the conversations, and he asks questions and raises issues that coincide with those asked by the play. The dramaturg defines this role as a chance to contribute to the depth of the director's contemplation about theme and meaning.

A different dramaturg defines this relationship as one where she reflects the ideas of the director. The conversations are held after rehearsal and she prompts the director to ruminate on the thematic issues in light of the work that was done. She responds by restating and helping to solidify the thematic points that the director raises and uses her knowledge and research to further bolster those meanings.

We require more from our defining than setting expectations and clarifying roles. Definition is the first step of the process to dramaturg, and the first thing to do at the onset of any kind of project is to identify and define the parameters of that project. It is the starting point of the dramaturgical work and one that is specific to the given project. Each new play, production, element of production or any project the dramaturg tackles has this stage in which the essential nature of the work is clearly parsed and articulated. Defining is to make clear and distinct; the first stage of the dramaturgical process is to discover the clear and distinct parameters of the work to be dramaturged.

Example: Dramaturg as Researcher

Dramaturgy is most frequently associated with production dramaturgy on an existing text and the task most often considered is the task of research. A dramaturg researches. However, this requires definition as much as any other project. What are the kinds of things that need to be researched and to what end? For whom are you doing the research? The dramaturg has to begin by defining the scope and context of the research he is doing. The research needs to be useful and related to the production at hand in order to be effective. A contemporary adaptation of Shakespeare's Much Ado About Nothing *is likely not going to make use of much research on the conditions and community of sixteenth-century Sicily. However, a close reading of what is happening in the contemporary community in which the play is being presented may be very useful.*

On another production, a dramaturg is working on a movement-based silent piece. The collaborators do not need support in the research on movement or story. Instead, the dramaturg begins to explore cognitive response to silence and audience reception to silent narratives. He becomes familiar with the theory around the kind of work the performance is seeking to achieve as a way to contribute to its effective creation.

Defining is a dynamic activity, and this stage of the process requires the dramaturg to have a focused and attentive approach. Defining the project seems like a simple and straightforward endeavor, and it is one that is paramount to the success of the work. While it is simple it is not necessarily easy and the act of defining requires the answer to many questions. What is it? What is it not? What is the goal? Who is it for? What are the constraints? What are the demands? A clear sense of the purpose and the goal of the project is fundamental to the ability to define it; consequently, the dramaturg needs to be diligent about the function of his project. There is not room in the process to dramaturg an element of production in a vacuum; each piece is always part of the whole and the parameters set for the piece are shaped, in part, with regards to the whole.

Example: Dramaturg as Audience Outreach

As part of the production process, the dramaturg may work with a marketing department, or in lieu of a department, on audience outreach. The primary intent is to get people to see the show, but more generally is an

(continued)

(continued)

early point of contact with the intended audience that may influence their experience of the production. Audience outreach is a way to connect to the various groups you hope to contact as well as to offer the various types of information and ideas about the performance.

For instance, a theatre is doing a series of short plays about sexual violence in a city with a large number of colleges. The dramaturg recognizes the opportunity to join the conversations about sexual assault on college campuses and reaches out directly to local schools. She uses some of the language and the imagery of the plays in order to evoke a reaction in potential audiences. She puts commentary about the play interspersed with headlines of real events and information about support for victims of assault in a deliberate mixture. She defines the outreach of this production as a public service announcement to and a voice for a population that is often marked by sexual violence.

When we define the project, we conceptually draw a line around what it is in order to separate it from what it is not. Each work requires a different criterion and that particularity is what allows us to draw a distinct line around the project. Chapter 7 will look specifically at how this can be done for particular elements; however, it is useful to note that it is through the act of selection that the shape is revealed. Determining what the project is helps to specify what it is, and this identity will be identified most directly through its purpose. Once we understand what the element needs to do, we can select in order to make it clear and distinct, and also particular. An important aspect of this process of definition is that it gives a particular identity to the project; it stops being of a kind and becomes a specific and definitive entity.

Once the project is clearly articulated, through its function and its constituent parts, the dramaturg solidifies his understanding of where this project fits into the larger context. If it is a production element he looks to the production as a whole, if it is the production he looks to the season, the work of this theatre in relation to those surrounding it or the particularity of this event in the context of the related events surrounding it. The process of the dramaturg is one that recognizes its place in other processes.

Step 2: Gather the Content

When the project is defined the next step is to find the content that will inform it. This is the "research" phase, a vital step in the production, which often becomes the visible task most frequently associated with dramaturgy. However, that association often comes with the assumption that dramaturgical research is essentially merely fact-finding. The task most widely understood is that the dramaturg is the person who will define terms, look up historical data, and answer specific questions that arise from the text. These things are often part of the task of dramaturgy but are merely a part of the content discovery that we do when we dramaturg. The collection of data is something that everyone on the production is doing throughout the process, and the role of the dramaturg can help streamline that process, but is not the aspect that characterizes the contribution dramaturgy can make to a production.

Gathering the content is dependent on the project defined, and it is the clarity of that definition that allows for the specified, targeted research that is so important to a dramaturg. She is working on production time, so the time spent uncovering content needs to be well used. The content is found in a variety of places and can consist of virtually any material that will contribute to the project. Written text, visual imagery, experts, case studies, objects or experiences can all be used to help shape the experience for the audience.

The content is determined by the definition reached, and we seek out the answers to the questions that need answers in this particular venture. Although there are some general guidelines for certain kinds of content, for example a glossary, there is nothing general about the content we compile for it. The particularity of the definition of the project is what allows the specificity of the content. When we know precisely what it is that we are making, it is much easier to determine the building materials for it.

Content discovery is an important part of play production and, while each member of the production team is gathering the information they need for their individual role, the dramaturg may find additional avenues and overlapping circumstances that will be useful to the rest of the production team. A glossary is a common tool for the production and is most often compiled by the dramaturg to complement the fact-finding done by the other artists. A glossary will include pronunciation and definition and context of unfamiliar words and references, but it is the research that is particular to the production that is most useful. It is the content that shapes the staging of the play, that adds to the composition of the production that is most useful as dramaturgical input.

Example: Research Scenarios

The facts that are gathered give context; however, the meaning of the context is most often what is useful. A character is offered a certain amount of money to kill someone, and he seriously considers the offer. This is information about the character, and further information into that character becomes more specific by the amount offered. The characterization of one who stops to think about it for $5,000 is different than that of one who does the same for $100. Even more so, when the amount of money is understood in terms relative to the character – is it more money than he would see in a year, or just a convenient excuse for a killing? This is a kind of dramaturgical research that goes past the simple conversion of currency from one time and place to another to understanding the significance of the context and providing an actor character-information through the research.

A dramaturg who is looking at cultural customs for a period piece discovers that it was considered unlucky to say goodbye in a doorway. She brings this information to the director, who then stages an emotional farewell between lovers on the other side of the stage, away from the doorway, and the scene ultimately benefits from the expanded tension of the character's long exit after the final goodbye.

Content can be broad and is often more useful when it pushes past expected sources and forms. One of the primary uses of flexible thinking as a dramaturg is in research, where we can approach subjects with a creative mindset that can take us in interesting directions with the form as well as the content. The questions we ask and answer need to be connected to purpose and use; however, a constructed artifact in the rehearsal room or a series of photographs or music in a dark room can be effective kinds of content. Resources do exist online and in libraries but those are not the only, and sometimes are not the best, sources for content for the project. Sometimes the most useful content is an experience.

Example: Content as Experience

The dramaturg brought the company together and turned off the lights and told ghost stories. The tone of the production was creepy and suspenseful and he wanted to remind the cast what that kind of tension felt like, and how it changed the quality of an experience. The cast experienced the ways their voices changed with the telling of the story, the increase of the heart rate in a moment of suspense and the expulsion of breath and nervous laughter around revelations. The dramaturg wanted them to experience the way the group checked in with each other, looked around to reinforce the sense of a shared experience. Telling ghost stories in a dark theatre was done to show the company the mood they were hoping to inspire in their audience, and remind them it was a precarious kind of tension that needs to be balanced.

It can be vicarious experience as well. In a play about drug addiction, the dramaturg brought in guests who were able to talk about their own physical and psychological experiences with drug use. The guests were able to give a specific and firsthand account that the actors could use as a point of reference in their work, as well as answer technical, physical movement, and emotional questions.

Another way that the content collection is driven by a clearly defined project is that it will be sought based on the expectations of its specific needs. When the first step is done effectively and it is clear what the project is and is not, gathering the content will have a much clearer vantage point. Without that clarity, a dramaturg can end up spending a lot of wasted time seeking out pieces that are not going to be useful to the particular venture. Dramaturgy utilizes directed, specific, process-driven research. It is content that is sought and collected in order to directly affect the project, whatever that may be.

Once the kind of content is identified and the content gathered, it must be edited. It is an important aspect of this second step in the process. The dramaturgical content is not just a large collection of content that is stacked up and left in a corner to be perused when inspiration comes. The purpose-driven content must then be synthesized in such a way that sharpens the specificity of the dramaturgy while keeping away any extraneous information.

The fundamental requirement is that the content be useful and so it needs to be a reasonable amount in order to be used. In addition, we include only the pieces that are of utmost relevance. We may find some interesting and entertaining ancillary materials; however, we need to keep in mind that the needs of the project drive the content and so we select only that which can be used. There are circumstances in which content that would seem secondary – and in fact would be in another project – are essential, based on the parameters of the project or the knowledge of the audience.

Example: Content for the Audience

The company specializes in classical work and is made up of an ensemble of history lovers. The dramaturg provides content for the actors that is text-heavy, with a fair bit of historical flavor. It is organized in a way that allows for easy access to further reading. She makes her own extensive research materials available to the cast before and after rehearsal and sets up time to have open-ended informal conversations about the historical period of the piece.

An actor got his first actor's packet and it was a three-inch, three-ring binder that was stuffed with articles, commentary, and timelines. It was significantly more text than the lines he needed to learn for his role. The binder made an effective doorstop and not remotely useful dramaturgy.

The process of content collection is not a fixed event, nor is it a static process. Collecting is a dynamic act with a flexible approach to the kinds of things that can offer useful content. This question of what can be useful is directly related to the project itself: what it is, what it needs to accomplish, and who is the targeted audience. Since those things are always different, the mode of collection is going to vary as much as the content itself. There is a collection of content, though it will take many different forms. The content is compiled, edited, and curated with the purpose in mind. Is it going to the actors or the production team? Will it ultimately be presented to an audience or is it perhaps for the archives of the theatre? Whatever the ultimate form, the content is gathered into some kind of collection. The overall goal of this step in the process is to discover, compile, and synthesize the most useful assortment of material for the precise requirements of a specific audience of a particular project.

Step 3: Communicate the Findings

Once the content is found and sorted, it needs to be delivered to those who can make use of it. The final step is just as important as the previous two, and it does not matter how well crafted the project and how useful the content if it is not presented in a way that makes it accessible and usable to its particular audience. Once again the specificity matters. While the presentation should be clean and easy to follow, well edited and well composed, there is no set way to present material. It can be in countless platforms: online, on paper, as a physical installation, a video presentation, or in any media that effectively conveys the content to the audience. The needs of the project direct the content-gathering, and they as deliberately shape the mode of communication. It would not be effective to use the same mode of presentation for vastly different needs and so the connection to "What is it, what is used for, and by whom?" is paramount to the design process. This can be something as simple as deciding between text and image, digital or paper, oral or written communication. It needs to fit the project as defined, leaving no doubt that it is the specific design for a specific project.

I have a friend whose motto is "If you are going to do it, design it." She is speaking mostly from an aesthetic perspective and asserts there is no reason not to take the time to create a deliberate composition of form with attention paid to aesthetic elements. The point extends beyond the aesthetics as well, and design also determines accessibility and usability. When it comes down to it, anything presented is designed to some degree; it may just be a question of "How deliberately crafted is that design?" Interactions with things are influenced by the composition of those things, and a meaningful design will help guide the process and shape the experience, and so it is a useful reminder when embarking on the final step in the dramaturgical process – communicate the findings.

Example: Content Delivery

Digital presentation of content can be useful for actors' packets and is an easily updated and eminently mobile mode of delivery. Online resources can be shared, they have embedded links to video, audio, and have other technical advantages. In one production, the dramaturg working with a

(continued)

(continued)

complicated script elected to use a web-based application for his materi-als. He created an interactive annotated script with pronunciation keys, images, musical clips and short question and answer prompts. In addition, he built an interactive map of the world of the play where the user could move through the virtual location on a platform that was reminiscent of a video game. It gave the actors a visual connection to the indicated places, and even indicated the relative proximity of offstage locations that were referenced.

The mode of presentation is also inextricably linked to the audience. Who we are speaking to is fundamental in determining what we say and how we say it. This is true in speech and writing, and is especially true in dramaturgical communication. If we as dramaturgs are preparing materials for an actor or director, the selection and annotation of material is completed and then the manner of transmission is directly connected to how that person/those people will use it – and from there we design it. The kind of content and the amount are going to be dependent on who we are assembling it for, and the mode of presentation is also going to rely on our understanding of our audience.

The choice of how to communicate is as important as the determination of what to communicate. Does it need words or pictures? Electronic or paper? Tactile or virtual? How is it spaced in terms of time and location? There are a variety of conditions that need to be considered since communication can incorporate virtually any mode that we can imagine. The goal is to construct the mode that will most effectively serve the target of our communication, so we hone in on the particular needs of that subject in order to shape our method of presentation.

Another way to consider this final stage is to look at this step as including an important and fundamental question: who is this for and what should it accomplish? That is a question that is useful throughout theatre management, and hopefully drives the work that is done across many departments. For the dramaturg, it is a way to remind us that the answer to the question has a concrete purpose.

Selecting the mode of communication relies on an understanding of both of these (interrelated) points of who it is for and what it accomplishes. A simple example is that the actor may need the answer to help flesh out a role, the designer to know what something should look like and the audience to understand a context. We have different points of access to each of those three subjects as well as the variation of the need and so we may offer significantly different information and use video, image, and text respectively to answer what seems at first glance to be essentially the same question.

Each project is changed by its mode of communication, and this final step allows for the ultimate efficacy of the project. Once the project is identified and data is collected, the precision with which the transfer of that information is crafted will be the ultimate tell of the usefulness of that which is dramaturged.

In summary, what is the purpose and who is it for? The answers to these questions provide the foundation of the three-step method to dramaturg and allow for the application of the mindset. When a project, or part of a project, is undertaken with clarity, flexibility, and a well-defined and clear purpose, it is much more likely that the outcome will be useful. A dramaturg who comes to the table with a holistic mindset and a purpose-driven process will be an effective creative collaborator.

Exercises

The purpose of these exercises is to build your skills of definition. These are aimed to require creative thinking and to reinforce the idea that the first step is definition.

Each of these activities should follow the three-step process:

1. Define the project; what does it mean to dramaturg this thing?
2. Collect and synthesize the content for that meaning.
3. Choose the platform to communicate the content and construct the output for a specific audience.

Dramaturg each one using the three-step process. Each should be clearly defined and constructed to be presented to a specific audience.

1. Dramaturg a song.
2. Dramaturg a place.
3. Dramaturg a person.
4. Dramaturg an event.
5. Dramaturg a collection – headlines, trending stories, YouTube screen.

7

THE SKILLSET IN PRODUCTION

The previous chapter outlined a method to apply the developed skillset to the work of the dramaturg. When dramaturgy as a way of seeing meets the tasks of the dramaturg the three-step process will prove useful to help develop the role and become a more effective artistic collaborator. This chapter will consider some of the typical tasks of the production dramaturg within the production team and examine ways to apply the mindset and method of approach. It first examines pre-production work and examines the process applied to the creation of the casebook. Then it continues with the rehearsal period and explores the dramaturg in rehearsal and during the rehearsal process. The next chapter will consider the following step, when the audience is engaged.

As previously discussed, the easiest – if not most effective – way to define the role of dramaturg is by the tasks of dramaturgy. The dramaturg is the person who does the research and compiles the actor's packet, the one who answers questions that come up in rehearsal. She offers context, asks questions, and it generally appears that the dramaturg is identified by the tasks she completes. As established earlier, the role is more than the sum of its tasks; however, that is the visible product of the dramaturg's contribution, and is a large part of what she brings to the production. The mindset to dramaturg is what makes those tasks valuable and that contribution more than merely the work product of the materials. In short, the approach to the task is what will ultimately determine its outcome, and the more solid the dramaturgical perspective, the more likely the content generated will be useful to the production.

The intent of this section is not to go through the tasks beat by beat; there are other places that offer a how to for these visible elements. The purpose of this chapter is to consider the various ways the shift in perspective and practice to dramaturg will serve the tasks associated with the role.

There are more resources and discussions happening about the role of dramaturgy in the American theatre than ever before, and we are in an exciting moment for the field. Some books and digital resources are available that provide step-by-step process for various tasks, including Scott Irelan, Anne Fletcher, and Julie Felise Dubiner's *The Process of Dramaturgy: A Handbook*, which brings the reader through the process of production work. In addition, Mark Bly's *The Production Notebooks* are an invaluable resource for emerging dramaturgs. There are informative dramaturgy blogs and a number of theatre companies publish their dramaturgical materials online for their audiences. This work is intended to join that discussion and look at the broader scope, to look at how the tasks can be integrated into a more cohesive kind of dramaturgy, to consider how they may be accomplished as part of the larger activity of dramaturgy. When the tasks of the dramaturg are refocused through the lens of dramaturg as verb, with flexible thinking and holistic understanding, their function can be better understood and their execution much more deliberate and precise.

The process of dramaturg as verb is one that works on the macro and the micro scale. It is a way to approach the whole production that helps to solidify the role and efficacy of the dramaturgy. The mindset and method are also ways to approach each project, each specific task. It is a frame for each individual task to help to shape the work into something that is allied directly to the needs of the production. When we define the parameters of the project, we do that for the whole picture – the forest, to revisit an earlier metaphor – as well as for the part on which we are focusing – the trees. It is useful as both a macro and a micro approach. This chapter will go through a couple of representative tasks of both pre-production and during the production process in order to further explore the approach of dramaturg as verb. The intent is to illustrate the application of the mindset and method to dramaturg.

As discussed in the last chapter, the question that creates the foundation for the work is this: what are we trying to accomplish and who is it for? This starting point shapes the three-step method and our ability to define the project – what do we hope to do? – as well as give context for the mode of communication – who is it for?

Pre-Production

The image of dramaturg as researcher primarily comes from the tasks she must undertake as a production dramaturg in the pre-production phase. It is this period of the production cycle – however long that is – that allows for time spent with the script and whichever members of the production team are already enlisted, in order to gain as much contextual understanding as possible. Some of this context will be shared directly with the production team through casebooks, websites, blogs, and presentations. The majority of this context will be used to create an understanding of the world of the play in order to be more fully invested in the world of the production and thus be a more effective dramaturg. The pre-production work includes research of many kinds that is about both the world of the play and the world of the production. Effective dramaturgy will come from the overlap of those two circumstances and so the dramaturg focuses her work as much as possible on the kinds of things that will be useful to the performance. For example, the better she understands why a playwright indicated a certain location, the more useful a resource she will be to help shape the visual landscape of the production.

First Things First: Script Analysis

One of the important early reads that a dramaturg makes is an analysis of the script. This includes reading for structure, genre, tone, story, character, and theme. The script analysis enables the dramaturg to delve into the text in ways that allow him to see the structural pillars that make up the story. He can piece together the clues that reveal character and the intimations of theme and metaphor. There are many approaches to script analysis that are effective and each dramaturg finds his own ways to approach the work.

What is the purpose? Who is it for? The purpose of the script analysis is familiarization with the text and it is for the dramaturg himself. Understanding the world of the play will allow the dramaturg to work with the production team on concocting the world of the production. The more familiarity he has with the workings of the script, the better prepared he will be for the first conversations with the director and designers to be meaningful ones. The questions and contributions will come from a place of understanding and the collaborators will start with a common source of information.

The method to dramaturg is pretty straightforward for script analysis. The dramaturg needs to be as familiar with the text as possible. The content gathered is a combination of the information mined from the text itself as well as the application of theoretical and stylistic models and any additional corollary information that will offer insight into the text. Finally, the mode of presentation is inherent in the process since the intended audience is the dramaturg herself. Consequently, the approach and format are determined by the dramaturg's own preferences and way of doing things.

Script analysis is a dry term for an exciting activity. It is the process of unlocking the character, of unwrapping the language, of revealing the texture of the play's world. The more scripts the dramaturg encounters, in text and on stage, the more versed he will be in this process. However, the flexible and open mind with which one approaches the text is extremely important. Even as the script analysis becomes a more familiar process, each new text needs to inspire the dramaturgical reading that takes it on its own terms and does not get bogged down in categorization or expectation.

There are two works that are a good inspiration to create a frame of reference on how to approach a script. One is Billy Collins' masterful poem "An Introduction to Poetry" where he asks the reader to look at poetry and "hold it up to the light/like a color slide/or press an ear against its hive." Mark Bly uses this poem when he works with young writers and dramaturgs and wrote a compelling article, "Pressing an Ear Against a Hive or New Play Explorations in the Twenty-First Century" that was published in *Theatre Topics* in 2003. Another source of inspiration on how to read a script is Elinor Fuchs's frequently cited essay "Visit to a Small Planet: Some Questions to Ask a Play." This is a widely used teaching tool for dramatic structure, and even more it is a piece that reminds us of the value of asking questions as artistic methodology. The idea is that script analysis is like dramaturgy in general; it is most effective when done with an open and flexible approach, and is responsive to what is presented rather that what is expected.

One insight that is constantly reinforced throughout theatrical work: the question and the answer are in the script. This is perhaps the most important concept for a dramaturg to keep in mind when working on a production with a script. The world of the play is created from the text, and all information about the rules of that world, the characters, narrative structure and theme all derive from that text. It is the common source material that all artists work from, and it is uniquely and specifically itself; consequently, the questions asked and answered for theatre-makers and audiences are going to come from the script. If there is a disagreement within the production team, the script is the most useful material from which to direct the conversation.

Another part of the pre-production work can be dubbed play analysis. This step coincides with the script work and consists of familiarizing oneself with the playwright, the theatrical moment, other productions, and the overall circumstances of the world of the play as well as the world in which the play was created. These are all elements that get the dramaturg as well acquainted with the text as possible, so when she has the opportunity to discuss the work with collaborators, she will have a solid foundation on the work as a starting point. Some of this initial research will be found in the later output to the production team; however, the purpose is a breadth of context and the audience continues to be oneself.

The next phase of the pre-production dramaturgical work is meeting with the artistic collaborators. Ideally this will be a series of in-person meetings to discuss the various ideas and questions that arise, whether in production meetings or one-on-ones, but the goal is to find out as much about the ideas for the world of the production as possible. Conversations with the director about the play are vital to help shape the dramaturgy.

The goals of the pre-production design meetings are to establish a clear line of communication, share resources, and to establish the conceptual explorations and decisions. The best preparation for this phase is a solid sense of the world of the play. The director and designers will have already done their own preliminary exploration of the play and will likely have some initial thoughts for the production. What the dramaturg can provide is a vocabulary for the production staff, a way to contextualize the work within the larger scope of the theatrical moment. His work naturally overlaps with the work of the designer and so the addition of visual materials can be useful. The dramaturg does not do the designers' contextual research for them, but brings in additional imagery and environment from the time and place of the play as a way to augment the conversation. In addition, the dramaturg helps maintain the through-line of the conversations as he navigates the conversations with designers, the director, and helps to ensure the collaborators are all familiar with the conceptual ideas that are decided or are being explored.

One of the reasons so many of the metaphors for dramaturgy are navigational is because it is a role that is dedicated to helping to bring the vision of the production to fruition. One way to help that happen is to have a very clear understanding of where the production wants to end so the dramaturg can determine the steps needed to get there. The mapping or charting of a navigator seems an apt analogy for this function in the production. Whether she is charting by stars or smart-phone, the navigator relies on the specificity of the destination in order to determine the path. The dramaturg seeks a similar certitude in the conversations with director and designers to ensure she knows where the production is headed so she can help maintain the path. She helps to establish the vocabulary, listens closely and follows the path of the conversations that happen and the decisions made to ensure that they stay on course. In the event that they veer, she is able to ask the questions and refer to earlier choices in order to help collaborators stay on path, or agree on a new one.

While the overall viewpoint and role in collaboration seems to be applicable to any situation, the work of the dramaturg is not without specificity and the tasks of the dramaturg are connected to the specific production. The script analysis one does for oneself is connected directly to the text as written, the content one offers to the production team links to the script as text for performance. Periodically the question arises about sharing the research from a play. Once a casebook is created, why not circulate it? Is that not a dramaturgical task completed? While there are elements that are somewhat standard, this way of thinking minimizes the contribution that a dramaturg makes to a production. The casebook is generally a compilation of information about the playwright, production history, as well as terms, places, and ideas within the play. The idea that it is transferable alludes to the task of assembling data to access as the creation of a casebook. However, effective dramaturgy will be particular to the production so will not be readily recycled for another.

Approaching the role and the tasks with the mindset to dramaturg will help shape the work into something specific and useful. Understanding the process of production, thinking flexibly, recognizing timing and connecting to the play and the audience creates the context for a dramaturgical output that is vital to the production. When this mindset is met with the process to dramaturg applied to its tasks, the creative collaboration of dramaturgy is most likely to be realized.

The Task: The Casebook – a Tool for a Well-Resourced Production

The casebook or the dramaturg's book are among the names used to describe a document that is created in order to capture the contextual materials and make the content of the script readily available to the creative team. The version that goes to the actors, typically called the actor's packet, is often an abridged version of the casebook and with character-specific content. The casebook is typically seen as an in-rehearsal resource and a repository of information that may be needed through the rehearsal process. Other members of the creative team also often use it, though it is generally constructed with the actor in mind. While this task, as the others, is largely dependent on the needs of the specific show, there are some common content areas that are present in the casebook. The casebook may include:

- playwright information;
- production history;
- glossary;
- character information;
- social/political/historical contex;t
- theory/criticism;
- visual imagery;
- theoretical or philosophical issues.

There will be other categories for other casebooks. In general, however, clarification of language and references will show in a glossary and information about the playwright, the world of the play and the world of the playwright will be present. The approach to the casebook will help to determine how these categories are treated and how useful this "book" will be.

The casebook is a significant opportunity for effective dramaturgy and is a useful repository of valuable information. The nature of that information and the manner in which it is presented are the two most important determiners of its likely usability. To start, define the project. Some of the questions that will inform this definition include the following:

- What function does the casebook need to serve?
- When in the process will it be available?
- How will it be used?
- Who is it for?
- What other sources of information will it be joining?

Once the general needs are identified – particular to the specific audience – the casebook can be defined and outlined.

A good casebook is a functional and valuable tool for actors, designers, and directors. It is a repository of content that can be sourced for actors' packets or image archive. In short, a well-executed casebook contributes to the production. If the content is difficult to use or the presentation is offputting, the packet may be ignored. An actor friend tells the story of the extensive book he was given at the first read-through for a production of a tough role. It was color-coated and cross-referenced, was beautifully formatted and was hundreds of pages long. The first article was a complete academic journal article with complex and dense theory. The actor brought the binder home and promptly forgot about it while he started his work on the role. It is a good reminder for a dramaturg and highlights the importance of understanding what any given task needs to accomplish and who it is for. A giant binder full of information does not seem as if it would often be a useful handoff to an actor. He is concerned with characterization and lines and the research he is doing for character, and the casebook needs to be something that will complement that work, and be useful to that actor.

The audience of the casebook determines what it entails, how much detail is necessary and possible, and what it is possible to assume is known versus needs to be articulated. The actors' books will be customized to them. Sometimes this will be a case of the age and experience of the actors, sometimes the relative popularity of the play or playwright, and other times there may be a regional difference that helps to drive the demands of the casebook. For example, if there are regional practices or references in a text, their context is only necessary to someone unfamiliar with that region – this could be terminology, like a liquor store is called a "packie" in Boston, or can be a practice like eating black-eyed peas on New Year in Texas. It reinforces the importance of the dramaturgy being connected specifically to a production and not generically to a play. The casebook is for the creative team on the specific version of the play with whatever adaptation, concept, and company that implies. Consequently, all choices about what to include will be predicated on those circumstances, and the project is defined by that standard.

At this point, the dramaturgy goes back to the stage of definition for each of the content areas that will make up the packet. The individual sections require as specific an approach as the whole work in order to be pertinent and useful to the production. Each element needs its own purpose and direct correlation to the whole.

Some Elements of the Casebook

The playwright biography tells the creative team the parts of her life that offer insight for the production and the production history creates a narrative to contextualize the play in performance. The pertinence and value of a casebook are determined by the purpose it serves. Understanding the world in which the playwright created the piece can help unlock some of the content, and knowing where she is coming from in terms of her own personal history, political leanings, education, family, are ways to contextualize the things about which she writes and offer further insight into story and character. The playwright biography is not meant to be a *Who's Who* entry, and its adherence to the needs of the production team will be what keeps it useful. The given circumstances of the playwright are going to be a useful tool for the dramaturg's own context, and elements of it can be pertinent in a casebook. It is not necessary to draw conclusions about the play or make assumptions about a playwright's personal life connecting to a work; however, this fleshing out of the writer can shed light on aspects of the play or at least introduce a way to discuss them. Similarly, where a play fits into the body of a writer's work can contribute to the approach to a work.

For example, the importance of biography can be seen in Sarah Ruhl's *Eurydice*, which was inspired by the death of her father; this gives some context to the addition of the father in the play and offers insight into the changes made from the original myth. Similarly, the autobiographical aspects in the works of Tennessee Williams provide character information and help to reveal some of the dramatic tension in the works. The play within the body of work is a significant key to understanding August Wilson's Century Cycle and how each play fits into this larger project looking at questions of power and identity for African Americans in the twentieth century. Or a different kind of context can be seen in Henrik Ibsen's *An Enemy of the People*, which was written as a response to the criticism of his play *Ghosts*. The biographical information on each of these writers helps clarify the meaning and intent of the action of the play as well as giving the creative team more conceptual input for the production.

Production history is another category that can easily become a chronicle rather than a commentary. While the initial perusal is to get a sense of where and when the work was performed, what kinds of venues and what kinds of responses, it is only the narrative of that production history that warrants placement in the casebook. Once again, the need to define the project and identify its purpose is evident. Are there points of interest about the reception to the play or the manner in which it was presented in other productions that can enhance the understanding of the play or its potential impact on audiences? Are there anecdotes or trends that will offer insight into the work of this particular production? Is there a story to a production history that helps the production team tell its story?

Information about the playwright and production history will usually be of use to the dramaturg when he is familiarizing himself with the play, and these categories of information will often find their way into the casebook and actor's packet. These are useful inclusions when their purpose is clear and well defined and they are part of a well-conceived whole.

Perhaps the most widespread component to the actor's packet is the glossary. It is a document that will include words to define, pronunciation, locations, references to explain and anything else in the text that is likely to warrant explanation. Glossaries are well-organized, quick references that are incredibly beneficial early in the production process. The defining of this task really is about selection: what are the words/ideas that need to be included and what can be taken as general knowledge? How much detail is useful and how can it be integrated into the rest of the casebook?

The most important rule of the glossary is that it must be usable, and generally needs to be an "at-a-glance" resource that is compiled based on what the actor needs to know. There is no fixed metric for what to include in the glossary; however, here are some guidelines to consider:

- Pronunciation: Name or word in a different language than that spoken in the play; name not in common usage to the region of the production; names of places not in common usage.
- Definitions: Complex vocabulary not in common usage; industry-specific terms and lingo; slang or dialect terms.
- Locations: Ideally include maps and descriptions of places real and imagined, referenced in the play.
- References: Examples of works of art, movements, styles referenced in the play.
- Context: Historical references, places, battles, periods; philosophical movements; political or social ideology.

Character information, cultural context, genre, and criticism all have their place in some casebooks. Once again, the need to define the project is paramount. Once the dramaturg determines the nature of the casebook and what it is meant to provide, she will select the areas that need to be addressed. This definition will come in part from the needs of the play and in equal measure from the thrust of the production. If the director is taking a certain approach to a work, the casebook will require attention being paid to the issues surrounding that approach – if it is a psychological bent or a Marxist read or a traveling sideshow, the casebook reveals the production as well as the play.

The first step of the process to dramaturg is to define the project, and when the casebook is defined, step two is the gathering of content. This is a huge process in the task of the dramaturg and the reason that "researcher" is something that is so closely associated with dramaturgy is because that is a large portion of the role. However, we also need to look closely at what it means to conduct dramaturgical research. There is the component that is looking things up in books and online, finding specific information to answer particular questions. Much of the glossary, for example, is going to be the concrete data that is found within the traditional modes of research. The dramaturgical mindset allows for an approach to research that both expands its boundaries and also looks to content-gathering as a way to open conversation and broaden perspectives as much as find new avenues of information-seeking.

A useful casebook is an example of how the mindset to dramaturg can open the conversation and directly contribute to the artistic development. A casebook can start a line of inquiry by including not only a painting that is referenced in the play but also the artistic movement that spawned it. Perhaps the character makes reference to the painting as being the first time the artist received critical acclaim, and it was at the beginning of an artistic movement that transformed the field and created a new approach to technique. The hope and energy of that reference is something that would inform the character for the actor, and could inspire a conceptual direction for the collaborators.

Another way the conversation can be expanded would be incorporating a brief biography of a person on whom a character is based while also providing a short context on how that person has been portrayed in the press. This depth of information offers the creative collaborators a point of reference on why a dramatic choice has been made so as to better execute the presentation of that story. A function of the casebook is often to create context of the time in which the play occurs, and sometimes it is the music, architecture, street art, video games, or the graphic novels from the period that will open up the play for the collaborators in a way that allows the work to flourish. Framing the casebook within its intended goal, and having the flexibility to allow room to include content that accomplishes that goal, will help to make the dramaturgy effective and the output useful.

A way that the flexible thinking of the mindset is exercised is through the avenues of research. While the traditional modes are useful and offer a lot of possibilities, the need-driven research of dramaturgy often inspires unusual sources of research. Whether it is personal interviews, boxes in an attic, a poster at a boxing gym, the medieval torture museum, techno-pop from the 1980s, a dollar store or hand-drawn maps of Middle-earth, the source material for a dramaturg is anything that can offer context. It is the culmination of what she is able to see and hear and ultimately connect into a usable form to share with collaborators.

The dramaturg's ability to select and synthesize is as important as her ability to find content. There are many interesting avenues of inquiry and a whole selection of content areas, yet if one hands over a thousand pages of essays, articles, and images, the casebook will unlikely even make an effective doorstop. The key is efficacy, and the packet must be useful for those who will do something with it. It needs to help the actor play a character, help the designer create the landscape of the play, and help the director shape the world of the production.

Once the content areas are identified and the content gathered, the process of editing and creating the narrative begins. It is specific, research-with-intent and the synthesis of the materials reflects the intent. Ideally there is a combination of media represented, visual, aural, as well as text-based offerings. Whatever the makeup of the content, an essential element of the dramaturging is the synthesis of that content. The usefulness of the substance of the casebook will be further shaped by the effectiveness of its editing and the clarity of its presentation.

Communicating the Casebook

The third step in the formation of the casebook is its composition. As stated earlier, the effectiveness of dramaturgical output is reliant on all three steps being executed well, and the casebook definitely relies on its successful presentation. This section will look at the way the communication is determined and a couple of options for how to present. The mode of presentation is as connected to the "who" as any other element. "What function will it serve and who is it for?" This is a question that bears repeating because it is one that is fundamental to the dramaturg's tasks, and will be at the forefront of the decision how best to communicate the findings. The terms actor's packet and casebook imply a physical object, a printed and reproduced book that can be flipped through at rehearsal. However, many dramaturgs now elect to practice a kind of digital dramaturgy and use combinations of online platforms to share their findings. These can take a variety of forms, websites or blogs, or repository-based platforms like Pinterest or Tumblr.

A chief characteristic of dramaturg as verb is that it consistently evaluates its own mode of operation, and the constantly evolving nature of digital dramaturgy is a natural ally to that process. The constant defining, compiling, and composing that is dramaturgy meets the ever-shifting process of digital communication in an exciting way. There is some interesting and exciting work generated in that intersection.

Digital dramaturgy is not the only mode of communication, nor is it necessarily the most successful. The goal is to find the most effective way to communicate your content – in a way that makes it usable – to your audience. The digital platform has some real advantages, starting with the fact that it is accessible whenever the user chooses. The proliferation of smartphones means a person does not even need to wait until he is at a computer to access his actor's packet. The platform allows for much easier inclusion of other media, especially video which can be a valuable resource. Printing and reproducing expenses and time are eliminated and the process to change and disseminate the content is much easier than with a physical casebook. Finally, it is the mode that most of our audience in the creative team are accustomed to using. The comfort with which digital media is navigated is something that definitely affects the decisions to utilize it.

It is the comfort of digital platforms that may drive the dramaturg to elect to find another mode of communication. The challenge with a digital-drenched audience is the question of how much of that media they absorb. If the casebook is glanced at with the same half-attention as the twitter feed, it may not be as usable for the actor. That is assuming that it is looked at in general. If the creative collaborators do not start off with the perspective that the casebook is going to be useful to their process, it may be more of a challenge to get them to participate in it, especially when it is so casually easy to access. It seems counterintuitive; however, the fact that the familiar starts to become invisible is not a new phenomenon, and some dramaturgs are electing to reintroduce the physical artifact into the rehearsal room to make it visible.

The physical casebook does not need to be a large three-ring binder with color tabs, nor does it preclude a digital presence. What it does is give the artistic team an object to physically interact with, which can be a useful component to the dramaturgical book. The point is that the content determines the medium, as do the audience and the purpose. It is the clarity of these in combination that reveals what the mode of communication needs. Perhaps a presentation at the read-through with some visual materials and a link to an up-to-the-minute dynamic and comprehensive blog will be the most useful. Or an accordion board in the rehearsal hall that has new arrangements of thematic content assembled for each rehearsal. Maybe audio played before and after rehearsal or a fully annotated digital script with interactive maps and iconography. The dramaturgy is effective when it is useful, and the dramaturg elects a mode of transmission that he thinks will support that mission.

The success of the casebook is revealed through its use as a tool in the production. When the dramaturg understands the production and has a clear and specific goal for the casebook, gathers and synthesizes useful content, and selects a mode of communication that speaks to the content as well as the audience for it, the probability of that use is high. Each part of the casebook can be treated with the same methodological approach in order to be certain the content is necessary and interesting and purpose-driven.

The Task: The Dramaturg in Rehearsal

The dramaturg's role in rehearsal changes from one production to the next, and also changes throughout the production timeline. Depending on how the director works with the rest of her creative team, the dramaturg may be a quiet observer in the rehearsal room whose contribution to the process is primarily in conversations outside the room. Or she can be one who is part of the discussion in rehearsal and asks and answers questions throughout the development of the piece. Communication may be via email or standing in the parking lot after rehearsal. What helps to increase the likelihood of a successful collaboration is that the expectations of the role are discussed and reconciled early and the dramaturg spends time in rehearsal.

The best resource the dramaturg in the room provides is herself. The information she has gathered, the connections made and conversations had are all part of that offering and it is also her taste and her attention and her response. It is important as a dramaturg to not underestimate the value of being in the room. You are watching what happens with the knowledge of what the production hopes to become, and you are seeing it when you are actively engaged to be responsive. This is a useful presence in the room and the key is to keep the communication that allows the production to benefit from this presence.

The role will change throughout the rehearsal process, and the earliest days of table work will likely be the time that the dramaturg engages most directly with the actors in rehearsal. The initial reads of the script generally include the introduction of the substance of the pre-production research, if not of the casebook itself. Questions of form and content often arise during table work, as well as larger conversations around theme and metaphor. The dramaturg answers the direct questions she can and makes note of those that arise, as well as participating in discussion of meaning and intent. Again, the way this occurs in rehearsal will reflect the agreement with the director about the preferred rehearsal protocol. While the actors are navigating the script, the dramaturg can help clarify questions as well as inspire ideas. When possible, it is useful to give a presentation of some kind to the company at the first rehearsal. This provides the opportunity to introduce the cast to some of the key thematic and contextual elements the production is enlisting, as well as an opportunity to introduce the presence of dramaturgy in the production. If it is a company with which one has worked before, or one with a history of utilizing dramaturgs, this step may not be as necessary. However, when working with a company that may not be as inclined, it is good to have the chance to introduce the kinds of work one can contribute and create the expectation of the work.

The specific goal for a process carries over to this phase of the production as well, and it can be helpful to have a particular goal for any given rehearsal. This is not the overall plan for the night the director may have, but instead a planned expectation for the dramaturgy. The plan may be related to story or character, such as: during this run I will track the progression of this character. Or it could relate to a metaphor or theme that is developing over time and the goal is to find the points in the play where it is made manifest for the audience. Frequently the goal of a rehearsal is checking for continuity. Whatever the specific project may be, it can help to block a rehearsal time for a specific purpose. In addition, the director may ask for a particular view or to look for something particular. You are in rehearsal to track the progress, recognize the stumbles, provide insight, ask and answer questions, and be the advocate for the eventual audience. All of these things require a close attention and openness to what is happening on the stage. The goal enables that openness to still be purpose-driven – not to narrow the vision but to give it a directional focus.

The dramaturg in rehearsal relies on the emphasis of timing discussed earlier. Understanding the flow of the rehearsal process is necessary to understand when a particular view is useful, and when a question or a comment is both useful and appropriate. Looking for continuity is an activity one engages in early in the process, and asking about nuanced emotional shifts is something that would likely come up toward the end of the rehearsal process.

Other tasks of the dramaturg take place during time not in the rehearsal room. Throughout the rehearsal process the dramaturg needs to communicate with the artistic collaborators, in production meetings and around rehearsal times. At these times it is important to ask questions and offer input into the production process. They also afford a valuable opportunity for the dramaturg to maintain contact with the individuals and processes with which she may not be as closely connected. For example, if costume design does not include as much contact with dramaturgy, the production meetings are a way to learn from that designer and keep track of the development of the aesthetic, and that point of contact could possibly identify a different avenue or opportunity to share images or materials that would benefit both departments. In addition, production meetings are a good way to hear the questions that arise and the modifications that are happening outside the rehearsal. The production meeting is not typically the venue for further exploration of dramaturgical output, but it helps to inform it and keep the connection to the whole creative team. The follow-up can then happen at another time or the dramaturg can get on the agenda for the next meeting.

Generally the most frequent communication in production dramaturgy is with the director, and for the most part the work that the dramaturg does with actors or other members of the creative team is cleared with the director. This relationship may be different in various production models and in dramaturgy done outside a traditional theatrical structure; however, the hierarchy of director as creative lead is most common. There is also a practical benefit to this open communication in making sure that the various elements are working toward the same production goal. If a dramaturg is doing one-on-one character work with an actor, she wants to be certain it is supporting the work that the director is doing with him in rehearsal. The best way to gain this assurance is through effective communication with the director.

Effective communication is one of the cornerstones of effective dramaturgy, and the in-rehearsal task of dramaturgy requires even more attention to the mode of communication. The dramaturg has to find the time and the manner of contact with the director in order to ask questions, offer input, and answer the questions she is charged with. Rehearsal time does not allow for this contact, for the most part, and so she needs to work within the production schedule and director's preference to find that workable space.

If the preferred mode is email, it can be a challenge to phrase things in a way that is clear and concise, and frequently dramaturgs make the choice to take a somewhat formal tone in writing so there is less chance of being misconstrued. An advantage to the exchange being in writing is that one has the opportunity to take the time to select one's words more precisely. However, there is limited opportunity for follow-up and there is not a measure for how clearly the director understands the question or comment.

Face-to-face communication allows for dynamic exchange and enables the dramaturg to observe the reaction to her words. It does not allow the careful word selection that writing does, but it creates a point of connection that can help to solidify the communication, and provides the opportunity to explain further or change tactics if the situation arises. The more time spent in the collaboration the easier it is to find the useful ways to communicate, and in any given situation the close attention to the needs of the show, a clear purpose to accomplish, and an understanding of your audience will be useful guides to how to proceed.

The dramaturg can answer questions, offer insight, track progress, and ask questions that assist the trajectory of the production throughout the rehearsal process, in and out of the room. In rehearsal, dramaturg as verb allows the dramaturg to approach with flexible thinking and a holistic approach, while maintaining a sense of purpose for the day and understanding the audience for the input. The casebook in whatever form it takes allows the artifact of the dramaturgy to be in the room, and the presence of the dramaturg provides the context, viewpoint, and response that she carries with her.

The biggest asset of the dramaturg is his active and engaged presence. He brings with him the script analysis, the research, thought, conversations and insight gathered from all of the time since the first day with the play. His attention to the process in and out of the rehearsal room give him a unique insight into the production and make him a useful presence in the room. This point of view also allows the necessary knowledge to be an effective contributor to the conversation with the audience and allows him to help to tell the story of the production.

A Schedule of Events

Production schedules vary at different theatres, and the dramaturg's schedule must coincide with the fixed dates and typical practices of the company with which she is working. However, it is useful to consider a typical schedule of events for a production dramaturg. The following is an example of a schedule for a production with a six-week rehearsal schedule and two-week run.

Pre-Production

3 months out: Hired as the dramaturg

> Read the script and did some preliminary research on the playwright and the play to familiarize myself with both. Did a brief production analysis of the text to get a sense of the production needs, structure, and style.

3 months out: Call with director

> The director was not in town yet so the first contact was a Skype call. We talked about the play, discussed her ideas about the production and her expectations of the collaboration.

> After the call I started more directed research around the specific areas that came up in discussion.

2 months out: Production meeting

> This was a chance for the production team to meet and discuss initial ideas. I prepared and gave a brief presentation with information about the playwright's work and images regarding the world of the play.

> I began more in-depth research into the style, and some of the cultural questions from the text, and started gathering things for the casebook.

1 month out: First items of the casebook

> Sent some curated information to director and designers, coincided with a pending design deadline.

Production

Auditions: Attended auditions to see the kinds of things the director saw, and see what she explored in callbacks. Provided some visual images to use in callbacks.

Week 1:

>   First read-through of the script. I made a presentation to the cast and provided links to the initial casebook and blog.

>   During table work I worked through some questions and ideas and participated in the conversations.

Week 2:

>   Developed and circulated information for the press release.

Week 3:

>   Started public blog.

Weeks 2–4:

>   Met with director 30 minutes before each rehearsal to talk through the plans for the day.

>   Brought materials for company into rehearsal, made some readings available online and brought in books and collections of images to look through at break and after rehearsal.

>   Stayed around after rehearsal for informal discussions with actors.

Week 3:

>   Drafted the program note.

Week 4:

>   Actor field trip.

>   Designer check-ins to check on continuity.

>   Designed lobby display.

Week 5:

>   Attended run-throughs and gave more specific notes and made note of particular things to watch for.

Week 6:

> During technical rehearsals I watched for continuity and flow. Continued to meet with director.

> Load-in for lobby and designed talkbacks.

Week 7:

> Performances and the facilitated talkbacks.

Exercises

The purpose of these exercises is to practice creating some of the pieces of the materials that go to a production team.

To begin, select three plays for which you can access the script, including a well-known classic, a contemporary piece, and one with controversial subject matter. Use each play to work through the various elements of the standard casebook, paying particular attention to how they change with the different texts.

To develop the materials of the casebook, do the following exercises to refine the work with the following prompts. Be sure to have a specific audience in mind and gear each exercise to that audience.

The Materials of the Dramaturgy

1. Use the well-known classic and create the playwright biography, theoretical framework, and glossary.
2. Create three versions of a glossary for the classic play using three different media.
3. Create a presentation for the design team on the contemporary play.
4. Consider the play with a controversial subject and design a visual display for the rehearsal room.
5. Plan a series of activities for the cast for the play with controversial subject matter that would help build understanding of the issue.
6. Design a speaker series for the company for the same play.

Scavenger Hunts

They are scavenger hunts because they are a search for specific information; however, the reason is not immediately evident in the question. The function of these hunts is to refine your research skills. These hunts will help to practice constructing content based on who it is for.

Determine how the content would be used in the production to guide the information gathered, and for each one, answer for (1) actor, (2) designer, (3) director, and (4) audience. The form and content should both change at least somewhat depending on the recipient.

1. The workplace doodles of famous mathematicians (Ptolemy, Alan Turing, Omar Khayyam, Amalie Emma Noether).
2. Drawing-room music (1950 London, 1890 Vienna, 1965 San Francisco, 1920 Paris).
3. Superstitions.
4. How to play a game (Texas Hold 'Em, Hazard, Go, Pig and Tongue).
5. Trails (Oregon Trail, Camino Inca, Appalachian, Trail of Tears).

8

DRAMATURGY TO ENHANCE AUDIENCE EXPERIENCE

Audience-directed dramaturgy is a significant part of the process and will be closely allied with the work that happens in pre-production as well as throughout the rehearsal process. The ideas, questions, images, and metaphors that inform the composition of the production are the same ones that will help to create the narrative of the audience outreach materials. The process of identifying, compiling and communicating the dramaturgy will allow for the work to be clear and specific and, hopefully, effective.

The work the dramaturg does during the rehearsal process is in preparation for the performances in more ways than one. First, she helps to shape the production into what is ultimately presented to an audience. In addition, she compiles information and a perspective that shapes the direct contact she has with the audience through dramaturgy's most identifiable tasks. The contact with the audience is where we can see the work of the dramaturg most directly, and when it is effective, the work can be an integral part of the production. It tells the story that will help to attract the audience, one that will both draw the best audiences for the piece, and prepare them for what they are going to see.

As the production approaches opening, the dramaturg's work is most visibly on display through the audience-geared work as it is usually a dramaturg who creates a lobby display and writes a program note. He is often recognized as the person who facilitates a talkback or coordinates a panel discussion. If there is an educational output, such as a study guide, that also tends to be tasked to the dramaturg unless an organization has a separate education department. Consequently, a fundamental aspect of the view of dramaturgy is the extra-performance contact with the audience.

The dramaturg is the advocate and surrogate for the audience during the rehearsal process. The advocacy serves two functions. It helps to shape the choices made in the production process and also indicates for the production what additional input the audience may benefit from. The purpose of audience-directed dramaturgy is not to explain what the audience sees, to tell them how to feel about it, or to defend the choices made by the production. Instead, the dramaturg's advocacy and later contact with the audience is a way to bring them more fully into the world of the play and give additional context that will add to the experience of the production. The audience outreach is a branch of the production, not an intermediary for it.

The dramaturg's contact with the audience may begin early in the production cycle and include contextual commentary in publicity plans and materials. Dramaturgical support can take many forms. In smaller companies and educational theatre it often includes assisting with audience outreach and publicity in addition to the production dramaturgy. The dramaturgy from the onset is connected to the "why this, here, now" and so the output can be a direct appeal to the intended theatrical audience, which makes for useful marketing materials. The dramaturg can help a marketing department by writing press releases or sharing images or content that informs the production and can potentially be useful outreach. For example, a well-executed website and production blog can provide effective audience engagement, especially for a targeted group or an established audience base.

A useful way to capture the production narrative is through a blog or a website, and this is something that is becoming a more common practice with dramaturgs. It is a way to chronicle the production life while it happens, as well as an opportunity to create the narrative record of the show. The dramaturg's written materials can also be the voice of the production team, the extra-performance commentary that can channel from production team to audience. It is an opportunity for outreach, advertisement, education, or discussion. At the same time, it is a line of communication that needs to be used deliberately so that it is an important part of the whole rather than a side note to the production.

Again, when there is a clear and specific purpose in mind, the shape of the dramaturgical output is much clearer. The audience outreach that aligns with marketing shares the end goal of bringing the audience into the theatre. Consequently, clear communication and a coherent plan are vital to the success of this collaboration as much as all the others. It is more than merely transmitting the materials from one department for use in another; the dramaturgy is deliberate and crafted to assist the marketing or publicity narrative in a way that serves the whole production. Whether it is in a season brochure or a press release, the first impressions that are transmitted can lay the foundation for a strong dialogue between the production and the audience.

When the dramaturgy is holistic and the artistic needs of the production are considered alongside the big picture the audience needs, the trajectory of the dramaturgy will be serving both from start to finish.

Once again, the mindset of the dramaturg enables the work to be deliberate and connected to the needs of the production, and the process allows the task of the dramaturg to stay relevant and useful. When approaching the tasks that connect directly to audience outreach, the emphasis on a specific purpose and the focus on particular targets will shape the work and increase the likelihood it will be effective. This can happen when the dramaturgy joins with marketing for publicity and outreach purposes and is seen more directly in the audience-specific tasks that are typically associated with dramaturgy.

Dramaturgy constructs a narrative, it tells a story of play-making in a variety of ways. It starts with a mindset as a way of seeing and engaging with material, it adopts a method that connects to purpose and intended audience, and ultimately it tells a story. The story told to the production team is the story of the text, and the story told to the audience is the story of the event. This story is told in a number of ways and it is essential that it offers a clear and comprehensible narrative. This chapter explores some of the tasks with which the dramaturg tells the audience the story of the production. They are noted in order of when they are experienced by the audience – lobby, note, talkback, and study guide.

The Task: Lobby Display

The lobby is an unusual place; in many locations it is a gathering and a waiting place. Whether there is an actual lobby space or a hallway outside the door to a black box, the transition from the world into the theatre is a threshold to cross and one that provides an opportunity for audience engagement. Threshold indicates something physical that is passed over as well as the point at which something changes. The lobby fits both of these images. Whatever space is designated as "lobby" is physically crossed over in order to enter the place of performance, and more profoundly, the transition into performance is inherently one in which something begins, or changes. The lobby is the space of that conversion.

There are a variety of different kinds of lobby displays, including an interactive display that allows the audience to post comments on a board, move pieces around a board, or try out dance steps. Another common form is an educational presentation in which things like timelines and maps may be used to illustrate the shifting demographics of a population, or the presentation of historical biography to present a context for the production. The display can be an opportunity for designers to present renderings, models, and inspirational materials, or it can be a chance to contextualize the world of the play in images and a compositional frame of reference for the audience to experience.

The lobby display is one of the opportunities the dramaturg has to prime the audience for the production. It is the literal threshold through which a person moves to transition from their world to the world of the play and the experience of that transition will affect the readiness with which an audience enters the production. Frequently the lobby display is used as an advertisement for a company or coming attractions, or sometimes it will be an educational display about a subject somehow related to the play or the production process itself. These can be interesting materials for the audience to peruse while they are waiting for the house to open; however, it seems like a squandered opportunity for a significant contact with the audience.

The first step to creating an effective and engaging lobby display is to determine what the lobby display needs to accomplish and for whom. Then location, resources, director's ideas, and budget need to be considered, as do the nature of the play and the production. Whether the lobby is a small corridor outside a studio space that requires the display to be set up and struck each day, or a self-contained and elaborate gathering space in a theatre lobby, the size and type of space is going to influence the kind of threshold constructed. The intent and design need to take into account the actual space that is used, and then figure out if and how to transform it.

The dramaturg works with collaborators to define the project – what is the lobby display going to be? How is the display going to coincide with the relative crowd and its movement? Is the audience required by traffic flow to move through or past the display or is it something that must be actively sought? What kinds of resources are available to support the creation of the lobby environment? These are all questions that point to the practical application of the display and they also contribute to the overall challenge of defining the project because it is something that will be largely defined by how it can be used.

If the purpose of the display is to educate the audience on a social or political issue that is addressed in the play, the character of the project will be defined by that educational impulse. For example, the display meant to introduce an audience to the circumstances surrounding civil war in the Congo may have maps and timelines, ethnic demographics and fighter mobilization. The display will include content about refugees and government corruption. The lobby will be composed in a way that not only offers the information about the situation, but can also give a visual and experiential feeling to that conflict.

In another instance, the historical context is selected to be an important educational opportunity; consequently, the display will be construed to serve that end. Court life may be the theme, and explanations of etiquette and stature will drive the display. The importance of pedigree and the visible displays of status may create the threshold into the playing space.

If the purpose is genuinely to bring the audience into the world of the play, then perhaps it will be an experiential display that allows for the materials of the world to be introduced to the audience in an interesting way. The audience may interact with the materials of a potlatch ceremony in order to create an ethnic and community feeling in preparation for the performance. Finally, the definition may reside on the need to engage the audience in a philosophical or theoretical process – to raise questions or ideas that will shape the way they look at the play. This kind of display can engage from an intellectual or emotional perspective and may include images and ideas that confront the audience members with troubling ideas, perhaps a presentation of eugenics or "ethnic cleansing."

Once the dramaturg knows what the lobby display is going to be, she can start the second step of gathering the materials. This part of the process happens differently than in some of the earlier production team-oriented tasks, in part because the lobby display is connected to the dramaturgy that has already happened. The compiling of material for the lobby is more a case of selecting and editing the dramaturgy from the production; finding the pieces that will help support the narrative of the display. What does it need to do, and who is it for? How can it prepare the audience for the experience of the production? What can it offer that will be meaningful at specific points in time, before the show, during the intermission, and after the production has concluded? These same questions shape the selection of material and will help to determine how much of what kind of thing will be most effective.

TIP: *Do not squander an audience.*

For audience engagement, there are generally up to three opportunities for effective use of this threshold of the world and the play. The audience uses the lobby before and after the production, as well as during an intermission if there is one. A holistic approach and flexible thinking are particularly useful for this construction, as is a sense of timing. Looking to tell a whole story in an interesting way, the dramaturg asks if there are ways to shape the experience going into the theatre, if there are equally effective ways to create an impression for the audience as they are exiting the theatre. In a production of Eugène Ionesco's absurdist play *Rhinocéros*, the carefully crafted lobby had been torn up, as if it had been trampled, when the audience left the theatre. The lobby was transformed into this mess while the spectators were in the theatre and it was a clever way to disorient the audience, bringing the world of the play out into their world. Similarly, a production of Jean Anouilh's *Antigone* in which the philosophical and moral argument was emphasized finished its commentary in the lobby where audiences were asked to drop a stone in a jar voting for which side was right, Créon or Antigone – or for those more inclined to contemporary resonance of the argument, audiences could also vote through #TeamCreon or #TeamAntigone. Once again, the timing was an important component and by choosing this activity at the end of the show, the audience was invited to be invested, to have a personal stake in the outcome of the debate, and to choose sides.

Making it personal for an audience is an effective way to inspire engagement, and dramaturgs often look for ways to use the lobby display as a way to connect to a specific challenge the play implies, or somehow place the audience into a point of view that may help them understand a character. There was a production that included a museum curator who had to choose which works of art to save before fleeing the country. The lobby display invited audience members to put a pin near the work they would save. It was an activity that the audience got very involved and invested in, though one that did not seem to have a strong effect on their experience of the play. The political and social implications of the destruction of the works ended up being a much more potent point of conversation in the after-play discussions. Similarly, in another section of the lobby, audience members were asked to identify what personal belonging they would choose once they knew family was safe. The lobby did an effective job of drawing people into the conversation about what to save, though the creative team was not sure it was ultimately as effective a mode of drawing the audience into the production. This question of making it personal comes up often, and sometimes we fall into the trap of thinking it has to be about our audience in order to be meaningful for them. Time and again we learn that is not a necessity, so even in our displays we can be sure to find the personal connection as one – but not the only – way to engage.

The final step in the process of this composition is selecting how to transmit the content. The materials selected for the lobby display are those that will support the purpose of the display. Some of the choices are practical – how much text should we use, how can images be included in a dynamic fashion, should we use digital media or construct a tactile experience? Is there enough space for the audience member to experience the display as intended? The mode of presentation needs to reflect that which is being presented and take into consideration who will be receiving it. The materials selected from the dramaturgy will not necessarily be presented in the same format to the audience. They are very different methods of connection with completely different purposes so it follows that there will be little about their presentation that will overlap. Something as simple as readability – even if the material is conveyed through text to both actors and audience, not only does the kind of content need to be modified, but the physical construction of it. How can it be readable in a case, or on a lobby board? If it is on a screen, how is that screen going to be integrated for the audience? The question of screens brings up another issue that dramaturgs are faced with in the composition of all of their output. Are our audiences so accustomed to the digital mode that they are essentially immune to screens and will they walk past a digital display without taking notice?

In addition, the narrative function of the communication is important to consider. It is not merely the practical consideration of the architecture of the lobby that affects the choice of form, but it is the desire to find the best mode of transmission for the material in order to convey the function. Again, the three steps are equally important and also inextricably linked. First, define the project, second, gather the content, and third, effectively communicate it. The defined project determines the selected content, which steers the manner in which it is conveyed.

A production of Peter Shaffer's *Equus* offered an evocative display that was in a self-contained space. Each audience member could enter and encounter numerous altars to modern worship. The space itself was deliberately claustrophobic with images of entertainment, consumerism, sex, and other cultural idols. It was chaotic and disorienting, and was an intriguing glimpse of the perspective of a disturbed character. Another intriguing aspect to this display was that it was an experience that had to be actively sought by the audience member. The display space was off to the side of the theatre lobby and even though there were signs notifying people they were allowed to explore it, it was dimly lit and appeared somehow illicit in its presentation, which reinforced the need for the audience member to choose to enter.

The mode of communication determines how the audience experiences the lobby display. Is it an immersive, participatory experience? Are there guided or free-form activities available in order to engage the audience directly with the materials? Do we have the audience making things, writing notes, trying out a tap routine? If so, the structure of the space needs to convey what is expected and allow for it to occur. This has a practical aspect in that we have to have enough room and enough materials for the size of our audience, but also includes the more ineffable: is the space constructed in a way that encourages an audience to take a risk, to do something outside the expected activity of moving through a lobby? Are there visual cues that tell people what is allowed and expected? Are there instructions, explicitly stated or implied, that let our audience know how to navigate this display? Is it something that is crafted in such a way that a person has to encounter the activity or immersion, or is it something that must be chosen?

The method of transmitting content is not merely how the information is crafted – text or picture – it is how the experience is shaped. It highlights the necessity of having a clear sense of the targeted audience because the cues must be clear to that specific group of people, and the experience needs to be fitting to their role. For example, there are times in which an almost hostile or confusion-inducing lobby display would be an effective preparation for a production; perhaps for a show about disorientation or displacement. However, if the audience is not primed for that kind of approach it could backfire and end up either losing them or bringing them into the production in a way that is aggressive or inflammatory. When the dramaturg understands what she wants to have happen, and who she is bringing in, she can temper the mode of communication to her audience. Often that will be merely a matter of degree; things that can be intimated for some audiences are better explicitly stated for others. Ideally these relationships are formed over time, and the more work a company does to intimately connect the lobby to the production, the more accommodating that audience becomes to those possibilities.

The lobby display in its most traditional form is a series of posters that offer a timeline and a text-based explanation – for example, a display consisting of posters with images and information about the Dust Bowl and its impact on the country presented in order to give the audience a context with which to understand *The Grapes of Wrath*. It can be well written with strong composition that allows the audience to learn something about the world of the play as a way to mark the threshold between their world and that of the characters. It can be seen coming in or going out and can provide an effective dramaturgical contribution. There are as many variations to the composition of the lobby as threshold as can be imagined, and decidedly non-traditional approaches may be suitable for certain plays, audiences, or spaces. The lobby display can be an opportunity to write on a wall, walk through a shower of torn-up letters, or peruse a carefully curated replication of a nineteenth-century doctor's office. It can be an activity that puts the audience into the place of a character in some way; for instance, they can be asked to choose what works of art they would save if they had to make that choice. The lobby display is just one of the places where the dramaturg tells the story of the production, and needs to be defined, compiled, and constructed. It will affect how the audience experiences the play since it is the point of crossing; consequently, it is a great opportunity to make it a significant one.

The Task: The Program Note

Like the lobby display, the program note is a direct point of contact between the production and the audience that is constructed by the dramaturg. This element is another visible contribution of the dramaturg, with authorial credit. The note is an opportunity to tell the story of the production and offer additional information or context to help shape the experience. The note connects the world of the play to the world of the audience. The program note is also an opportunity for the dramaturg to write an essay from her point of view. The note allows the space for a commentary about the world of the play and the production that the dramaturg wants to share with her audience. It is also a situation that is inherently challenging, since it is a voluntary act on the part of the audience member and may be read before the show, at intermission or at the end, depending on the individual. There is no way for the dramaturg to control the timing of the reading of the program note, when or even if it is read. Consequently, the note needs to be crafted in such a way that it is important but not vital information and is immediate but not linked to its timing.

> TIP: Remember the audience is a collection of individuals who will have a number of different responses.

The general rules apply. The program note needs to inform something about the play while not telling the audience what they are about to see or explaining artistic choices that should be allowed to speak for themselves. It needs to complement the director's note, if there is one, and any additional materials in the playbill. The program note gives some kind of insight into the production that will add to the audience experience and offer them a way to think about the play. Well articulated; with a fixed word count; to be read or not at the discretion of an audience member. It is not an insignificant challenge to construct an effective program note. The reality is that the program note is usually a thoughtful, well-researched essay that people will first read in five minutes while sitting in the dark.

For the dramaturg, the process is the same as with all the tasks. The first step is to identify and define the project. What does he want to accomplish with this note? What are the constraints with which he is working? There are a variety of things one can choose to attempt with a note. It is an opportunity to offer information on the time and place in which the play occurs or when it was written. The note can be the chance to share important information about the playwright or the production history. It can be used to discuss important thematic, philosophical, social or political issues raised in the play. The program note can do a lot of things, so the beginning is to determine what the specific note should do in order to define what it should be.

The notes are typically done pretty well in advance of the show to allow for whatever production process is needed and so this decision will often be made relatively early in the production dramaturgy. Consequently, it will frequently be connected to the content and point of view of the earlier part of the rehearsal process. This context and parameter form part of the understanding of how to write an effective note. The dramaturg can assume there will not be significant changes in the overall thrust of the play and so he can write a note based on the intent of the production, coupled with the content he has uncovered. While it is safe to assume no major changes, he needs to create the note with the understanding that some changes will likely occur. The project must be defined with its place in the production cycle in mind; and that place is unusual because it is created early on but will be experienced during the run of the show.

A variety of considerations go into the defining, including practical limitations and artistic desires, and ultimately a conclusion is reached. For example, a program note might offer a historical point of view of the world of the playwright in order to provide insight into the place from which the playwright created the piece. For instance, the play is a political farce that takes place in Italy in the 1970s, and so the program note is a historical essay on the political circumstances of Italy in the second half of the twentieth century. This type of program note is frequently adopted and has a clear purpose.

There are other kinds of program notes and other kinds of content the dramaturg may seek to communicate. The note may be a vocabulary lesson or a philosophical musing on the nature of a theme or metaphor from the play. It can be an exploration of the relevance of the play to the contemporary moment or to the theatrical movement. Whatever the form of the note, the style needs to be accessible and ideally suitable to the tone of the production.

Step two is compiling the content, which will generally come from the same materials collected in the casebook for the production team. The initial gathering of context cues that become the casebook and rehearsal materials provides the information, or at least the beginnings of the information, for the program note. At this point the challenge will be in editing and synthesizing the materials until there is something that can provide the spine for the narrative of the note. The key is to find enough information to create this historical frame, yet that is also interesting and can be transmitted through this short burst of a program note. Again, the different kinds of projects will require a different assembly of content in order to shape that specific note. A theoretical musing will demand something different than a historic timeline; however, the commonality is that the content will support the dramaturg's read of the play and production. The note is a way to speak to the audience, to tell a story of the process.

The project is defined, the content assembled, and the final step is to determine the mode of presentation. Once again there is a practical aspect: how much room is there in the playbill, what is the content of the director's note, and what additional content is present in the program? The practical will shape the delivery somewhat, but it will be more concretely influenced by the desire to target a specific audience and offer a particular experience. Much of the time the note will be a traditional text generated by the dramaturg and the style and structure of the writing is crafted in a way that links it to the mood and genre of the play, as well as reflecting the overall voice of the production. The word choice and theoretical connections are informed by the relative knowledge and sophistication of the audience, with the understanding that it will be read in the five minutes before curtain or skimmed at a later time. The style needs to encompass that.

Since the program note does not have to be a note, nor even necessarily in the program, the creative impulse of the dramaturg may extend past the essay format to create a visual collage or a pastiche of image and word. The form can be a pamphlet that is scattered through the space or a golden ticket under a seat. The purpose is to make the program note an effective point of connection with the audience, and the form it takes is integral to the connection. If it is something that the audience should read and/or see, the dramaturg needs to make sure it is constructed in a format that makes it visible and accessible to that particular audience. If it is not something the audience would derive value from, the dramaturg should save the ink. Like all dramaturgical output, the material needs to be effective, immediate, and necessary.

The program note is direct communication between the dramaturg and the theatre audience. It is a way to give more information, offer insight, ask questions, connect to metaphor, or engage the reader on a personal level. Once the dramaturg decides what he wants the note to be and defines the project, he can use the content he gathered in the early production phase and determine the most effective mode of communication for his specific audience. That process will allow him to stay connected to the overall thrust of the play and make effective use of this point of contact with the audience.

The Task: The Talkback

The dramaturg uses the lobby display and the program note to transmit information and ideas to the audience, and a third opportunity is the talkback, where he can have a conversation with them.

The audience talkback is a way to get direct feedback, create further conversation, and develop an audience. Talkbacks are particularly useful in educational outreach and in university theatres since they can help to teach an audience member how to articulate a response to performance. The term is used as a kind of umbrella for pre- and post-show talks of various kinds and may include a panel-style lecture with experts, a facilitated conversation among the audience, or a question and answer session with artists. They can be conducted for the benefit of a creative team, a playwright, an organization or an audience. Different kinds of talkbacks will offer different input and information to intended recipients, and the choice of what kind of talkback is largely determined by who it is meant to benefit.

The talkback is the extra-production opportunity to engage directly with the audience in an exchange rather than the one-way transmission of information. A well-crafted talkback gives the chance to speak about some of the decisions made in the production and to hear a direct response from an audience. A dramaturg can bring in experts from a particular field to help spark a conversation about the world of the play and the world of the production. The talkback can be the chance to hear a moderated response from an audience that has just experienced the show. It can ask questions, instigate discussion, answer questions, and give the audience something to think about. The talkback can be a way to garner community action, help rewrites, or shape future season planning. Ultimately the talkback provides an important occasion to listen, and when effective is enjoyable and important.

Talkbacks are often associated with those done as part of new-play development, and as such can be considered a somewhat sensitive dramaturgy task. Many playwrights do not like the practice and there is some contention over whether or not the audience response is a valuable contribution to the development of a play. This will be looked at in more detail in the next chapter.

From a dramaturgical perspective, pre- and post-show discussions are intended to increase audience engagement in the production. Whether it is to mine audience members' input as a way to inform the theatrical choices or to give a stronger sense of connection to the work, a company uses talkbacks to speak directly with the audience, and the challenge for the dramaturg is to make it a valuable and significant point of contact.

As with the other tasks of dramaturgy, the talkback is defined by a simple question: what is its purpose and for whom?

A pre-show talk is often a part of an educational outreach or sometimes is a special invitation to specific members of the audience. These talks may be used to invite people who are involved in issues surrounding the play and use the time to give the audience some context on the ideas they will see explored in the production. Or sometimes they are used as an opportunity to start the discussions that the production team hopes will be generated by the show. For example, a production of a play about three women in the Iraq War may invite experts on the region as well as on the political history in order to give the audience a stronger context on the circumstances of the play; and the dramaturg may bring in someone who can speak about the ways that gender plays a part in the circumstances of the play.

The post-show talkback is different in that it is usually an open invitation to any audience member who is in the room and will be an immediate response to what they have just seen. These talkbacks can also take many different forms and may include cast or production staff members in a question and answer format. One example of a post-show discussion is a variation of a pre-show format; the humanities-style lecture wherein the dramaturg assembles a panel of experts to discuss important facets of the play and production. Perhaps you bring in people to discuss important theatrical history and practice context, or you bring in someone who is experienced in a sociopolitical topic that is manifest in the show. The fundamental idea is that this format can give the audience even greater contextual understanding. Finally, a moderated audience response is another model of the post-show talkback. This way of engaging with the audience is less about offering context or information and more about giving the audience members the opportunity to speak about what they saw. A production of Lynn Nottage's *Ruined*, a play that deals with the ravages of war as played out on women's bodies, could be well served by a guided opportunity to articulate a response to the shared experience of seeing that story presented.

Production teams sometimes reject the idea of a talkback out of hand because the benefits are not clearly understood, likely because who and how the group would benefit has not been clearly identified. Important to note, the talkback generally benefits the audience more than the production staff, although there are occasions in which the production team will profit from the talkback. However, as the talkback occurs after the play is produced, talkbacks are to help future productions. Consequently, understanding who the audience is and what point of contact will be effective for them is at the core of defining the project. Talkbacks in university theatres are particularly successful, as they provide the opportunity to connect more directly to the educational aspects of the production. In addition, they can pull in other departments and fields of study and ultimately assist in furthering the mission of the department and the school.

Another popular type of post-show talkback is a "meet the artists" where the audience is welcomed to stay for a moderated conversation with members of the production team. These types of talkbacks can be done for any kind of show and tend to have an appeal based more on the process of the production and the personalities of the artists. Young audiences, in particular, enjoy conversing with the artists and having the opportunity to ask questions about their work, even though there is almost inevitably the question, "How did you learn all those lines?" Even still, these kinds of post-show discussions can be useful and informative about the play-making process, especially where there is a non-traditional approach to the work such as devised theatre.

The second step of the method to dramaturg is gathering the content, and for talkbacks that content is the people and the questions. Who are the experts to bring to the humanities-style panel? Can we assemble a dynamic group and people who can speak to the playing of the piece as well as their own areas of expertise? Are the styles and tones compatible, both with the other members on the panel and with the ethos of the company and the temperament of the audiences? Similarly, if it is a moderated response, what are the questions that will help guide the process while still having the room for an open-ended conversation?

Finally, the importance of the final step cannot be overestimated. What is the best way to accomplish this purpose and communicate with this audience? This stage also includes the practical ways the talk-back is framed and communicated. The dramaturgical output in this task is communication – the ability to listen as well as speak. Whether she is answering questions or asking them, the person who dramaturgs is one who is present and focused and able to respond to what she hears and sees.

There are some important practical guidelines when facilitating a talkback, including when and how to take the stage and even suggestions on how to deal with hecklers. The professionalism with which the talkback is advertised and framed helps the successful continuance of it. It is important to have open questions prepared in advance and then go off the pre-planned as soon as it becomes necessary to engage more fully in the moment. A thoughtful question or comment as well as a disruptive questioner can draw the dramaturg into the production further, though she will need to be sure to maintain the professionalism of her style and output.

The biggest asset a dramaturg can offer is himself, and understanding what that means is an important part of the process to finding the dramaturg's mindset. It is more than knowing strengths and weaknesses and styles, it is a way of seeing clearly one's own responses and allowing that to be the foundation of the work. Talkbacks give a particularly potent example of this importance because effective facilitating is done by people who have a clear purpose, target, and focus. Those elements are found in one's own style and approach.

A talkback leader at a regional theatre I frequent starts hers off by telling the audience the talkback is what we would do if we went out for a cup of coffee to talk about the play. She is warm and invites the audience to come and have a chat with her. It is a very effective mode of presentation and audiences quickly relax and participate in the conversation she helps create. Another local theatre has a talkback facilitator who is dynamic and energetic; he speaks quickly and exudes intelligence and wit and creates a lively discussion that energizes anyone who elects to stay and participate in the talkback. When the dramaturg elects to be himself and creates an environment based on his own style and personality, the talkback can be an exciting and useful activity. It touches all aspects of the event, including how to redirect a conversation or deal with an inappropriate or unusual line of questions. The audience responds more favorably to the comfort and confidence of being led by a prepared professional who is being oneself rather than trying to play a role based on a perceived notion of dramaturg as a formal, erudite intellectual or some such image. In addition, it creates a much more stable environment conducive to effective conversation.

When the dramaturg knows what the talkback needs to accomplish and defines the parameters with that in mind; when she compiles content that supports the specified goal; when she constructs a format that is complementary to the production, her own style, and considerate to the nature of the particular audience, that is when the talkback can be its most effective.

Tips for Facilitating a Post-Show Talkback

- Have a clear time frame – fifteen minutes is a good one – that is told to the audience and adhered to by the group.

- Prepare questions ahead of time. While it is important to be responsive to the direction the conversation takes, it is just as important to have some leading questions to start or restart the conversation.
- Come on to the stage immediately after curtain call and invite the audience to stay, then give two or three minutes to allow people to step out or move forward to join the conversation. Do not wait too long; people who are uncertain will not wait very long for it to begin.
- Call on people to speak. Even if the audience starts to respond to points made by another member of the audience, keep the organization of calling on speakers to maintain order in the conversation.
- Redirect speakers who go off-topic or try to dominate the conversation. This should be done politely and you must interrupt if necessary.
- Interrupt any speaker who becomes inappropriate and if there are artists on stage, refuse any questions that are not suitable to the context.
- Restate points made if the whole audience cannot hear the speaker.
- Listen. Pay close attention to what is being said and the overall tone of the talkback, and respond to what is happening in the moment.
- Be yourself. Use your own style to guide the conversation.
- End it. If the time is up or if the conversation is waning, thank them for staying and say goodbye.

In summary, the dramaturg answers the questions about the pre- and post-show talkbacks. What do we want the talkback to accomplish? In what way can it best serve the production and the audience? If we are in the very beginnings of creating a regular and invested audience, the primary function to develop that audience and give them some personal stake in the production seems a useful model. For a very complex play or one that deals with controversial and difficult subjects, the idea of bringing in experts and framing a more thoughtful conversation around those issues will make sense. Is there already an audience base that feels connected and entitled to the work? Are we seeking a new audience that needs some guidance? Then a talkback that is a well-guided conversation about their own response to the work will be well placed. Once again, close attention to "the who and the why" will determine the shape of "the what."

The Task: The Study Guide

The story of the production that the study guide tells is one that is meant to make the production as clear and meaningful as possible to a specific audience. Study guides are typically created for school programs and are supplemental materials for the curriculum the production is supporting. If there is an educational outreach program, the dramaturg is often involved in curricular support and may compile a study guide for the participating schools. The content and activities in the guide vary greatly depending on the grade levels and kinds of students who come to the productions. The study guide includes information about the play and the production process and suggests some topics of discussion as well as interactive activities that are age-appropriate. The study guide is a useful addition to educational programs in theatre and can help school groups increase the value of the experience.

Educational materials are relatively straightforward when it comes to informational content on the play and production; however, a holistic approach to dramaturg is useful to the creation of these as well in that it helps to shape the intent of the work. Knowing the audience is of utmost importance, age as well as experience with theatre, and this points to the kind of study guide to create. Clarity of purpose helps guide the work. The step of definition requires some choices to be made about the purpose of the study guide and the educational opportunity. Does it need to inform a well-educated student about the particulars of a theatrical movement? Is it an introduction to live theatre for a brand new audience? Is it an opportunity to inspire aspiring theatre-makers or lure future theatregoers? When the function is determined, the nature of the guide can be decided and the project defined.

Content will be compiled from the early work that oriented the dramaturg to the play and the additional output she created through the process. It will reflect the selected purpose so if the curriculum is based on introducing students to live theatre it will likely include information about designers and technicians and the overall process of play-making. The information about the playwright and the world of the play can be contextualized in a manner that highlights its identity as script for performance, furthering the connection to the process of production. Plot, character, thematic elements may be included, as well as any other contextual information that can support the project as defined.

The mode of presentation will depend on the audience and will be selected and written with regard to a particular age and perspective. The inclusion of non-text elements such as drawings, photos, or charts, as well as digital or interactive components, will all depend on the parameters of the project and the targeted audience. The starting point is to aid in the curriculum and engage the student audience. What those things mean, and how best to execute them, is how to dramaturg.

Educational outreach is an important part of the mission of many theatres and in some cases is connected to their funding. Theatre companies want to expand audiences and build the next generation of theatregoers, and outreach to schools is an effective way to accomplish these. It is a natural extension of the dramaturg's work and even theatres that have education departments tend to utilize dramaturgs in the creation of materials and execution of student outreach programs.

The effectiveness of educational outreach depends on finding the right audience for the work and creating a context that will make it a meaningful educational experience. The first part is dependent on understanding the play as well as having a strong frame of reference for what is appropriate and appealing to various age groups and then creating those relationships with schools that allow access. An educational department will be able to serve that role, in general, although even in a smaller theatre there is no reason to neglect the opportunity to reach out to a young audience for a production that may appeal.

The study guide will accompany the program. Once a school group is coming to the production, the dramaturg will schedule a pre- or post-show discussion that is appropriate to the show and group, and she will provide the students with her study guide. This document is as much an ambassador to the theatre as the dramaturg herself, so it needs to be engaging and well constructed and suitable to the particular audience.

Some Things a Study Guide May Include

- Information about playwright: who they were/are and where and when they wrote.
- Information about the play: summary of action, character, genre and style, glossary of terms, some production history.
- Information about the company: who is who on the production team, mission of company, reasons for selecting this show.

- Information about the process: how this play was made, images of renderings or other process-related materials.
- Activities: engage the student directly, exercises that connect the student to the play.

From the first read of a play through the final blog entry posted after the last performance, the dramaturg is working on multiple levels of contact with the audience. He reads the script with particular attention paid to what questions may arise for an audience seeing the play so he can make note of what to look for in rehearsal. He is the surrogate for the audience through the process of the rehearsal and build, helping to keep the show cohesive and ensure that the willing suspension of disbelief that is asked of the audience is also respected by the production. Finally, he works to shape the experience of the production for the audience, through pre-production communications and publicity, in the lobby, playbill, pre- and post-show conversation and any other opportunity to act as conduit between the audience and the production. The points of communication directly between dramaturg and audience are executed through the method and shaped by the mindset. Thus the dramaturg tells the story of the production.

Exercises

These exercises are intended to practice designing audience materials. Think about the kinds of ways these materials can be used to tell the story of the production. For each prompt, be sure to have a specific play as well as a particular theatre's audience.

Lobby Display

1. Design a portable lobby display without any text for a play by Shakespeare.
2. Map out an interactive display for a non-realistic play.
3. Design a lobby display for the last show you saw.

Talkback

1. Pick an "issue play" and plan a pre-show panel of speakers. Who do you have? What do they discuss?

2. Come up with six questions for an audience response talkback for the same play.
3. Plan a "meet the artists" talkback for young audiences.

Study Guide

1. Select an "American classic" and create a study guide for a high-school audience.
2. Revise for an international audience.
3. Create a study guide focusing on the process of the production.

Outreach

1. Write a press release about the issue play you selected for the talkback.
2. Design an advertising plan to get people interested in a contemporary play.
3. Create a plan for a direct appeal to a target audience.

9

DRAMATURGING NEW PLAYS
AND DEVISING

Dramaturgy is a theatrical process and one that can be an incredibly useful part of an artistic collaboration. While the mindset and process of dramaturg as verb are applicable to all aspects of life, this book has looked primarily at the traditional mode of theatrical dramaturgy, and the discussion up to this point has been anchored in production dramaturgy with an established script. That is merely one way that dramaturgy is applied in the theatre, and is the one used as the primary illustration because it is a widespread use and understanding of the role, and is effective to show the application of dramaturg as verb.

The premise of this book is that dramaturgy is a way of engaging with the world. It is not a collection of tasks, nor is it limited to a designated role in a production. It is a way of seeing and processing information and a mode of communication that is mindful and deliberate. Dramaturgy is not something that is relegated to a theatre, in location or activity. To dramaturg is to curate an experience for an audience. That can be done with any activity and any audience, and it is an expansive and encompassing way to understand the mindset and practice of dramaturgy. It is a way of perceiving and can happen all the time.

Dramaturgy as way of seeing is a particularly useful model when considering the various kinds of performance it encounters. Dramaturgy is practiced in dance, opera, and puppetry. It is seen in film, video games, and many other examples of performance and/or narrative expression and is a method that naturally joins many fields of study and practice. All of these applications can be served by the mindset and skillset to dramaturg. As a way to engage with materials and audience, the holistic viewpoint, flexible thinking, and responsive process make for effective collaboration. The scope of this book does not allow for an examination of each of these modes of dramaturgy; however, this chapter looks at two of the popular forums for work in the contemporary theatre: new plays and devised theatre.

New-Play Dramaturgy

The role of the dramaturg on a new play is to help facilitate the development of that play for the playwright, the festival, or the company. Whatever perspective from which she operates, institutional or personal, the new-play dramaturg can still exercise clarity of purpose, precision of content selection and synthesis, and efficacy of communication. She can be a creative artist in the room, an ally to the playwright, and a surrogate for the audience. In short, she can dramaturg.

Developing a strong relationship with collaborators is the most important aspect of working on new plays. The dramaturg may be there for an afternoon or a collaboration of many years and many plays with a given writer, and the result of that contact needs to be furthering the work of the playwright in a constructive and effective manner. It is an unusual working relationship in that the dramaturg is a creative collaborator but it is a support role. The dramaturg should have no personal creative agenda or personal stake in the work. The relationship is one that is dedicated to the vision of the playwright, and that is one that needs to be defined and redefined many times over the course of the collaboration. The dramaturg must help affirm that the common goal for all involved is for the playwright's play to be realized. Depending on the circumstances, this can mean a number of different things, and so clarity of purpose and goal is extremely important for an effective collaboration.

Through an active support process, the dramaturg can create an environment that is conducive to creative work, and ultimately that is the most important element of her work in new-play development. The ability to listen, respond, and communicate are put into play from the very beginning when working on a new play, and the more attuned she is to the needs of the play and the playwright, the more effective the creative environment will be.

One of the challenges of new-play dramaturgy derives from misunderstandings about the role of the dramaturg in new-play development.

Among the most damaging images of the dramaturg is that of "script doctor" which carries an implication that somehow the dramaturg will come swooping in to fix the script. This is damaging because it automatically creates an adversarial rather than collaborative relationship. The expectation is set that the dramaturg comes in as expert and authority, which is not at all conducive to a strong working relationship between writer and dramaturg. First, the script is not broken and does not need fixing any more than it is ill and in need of a doctor. Then, the person who knows more about a play than anyone else is the playwright, so the notion of someone else "fixing" it is problematic at best. Finally, the role of new-play dramaturgy is to listen, respond, and support the work and the collaborators.

The mindset to dramaturg is particularly useful in working with playwrights. Wherever they are in the process of developing a work, the holistic viewpoint and close attention to timing are particularly beneficial. The play is itself a process, so it is vital to understand what goes into that construction and the kinds of things that can be useful at different stages. A script in preparation for a first workshop read is a completely different thing than one being readied for its first production and the dramaturg needs to be connected to that circumstance. The questions the dramaturg asks and feedback she offers are likely going to be broader and more encompassing earlier in the process when the playwright is initially finding character voice and story structure.

> TIP: Do not look at the script when you are at a reading – pay attention to what you hear.

The circumstances will reveal where the play is in process and what kinds of questions the dramaturg is asking. For example, the first workshop read is typically a new script that is undergoing revisions, and those may be significant. This read is often done with minimal rehearsal and is generally just an opportunity to hear the work out loud. This is likely the first public reading of the play and the conversations between playwright and dramaturg may include large structural ideas, story arc or characterization. A play may go through this phase and come out on the other side with a new third act and having lost the love interest. A staged reading has a little more time and resources invested. This is typically a play further along and potentially ready for production. A theatre may do a staged reading in order to get a sense of audience reaction and overall workability of the script in order to determine whether or not to commit to producing it. Other places that are dedicated to play and playwright development may produce staged readings in order to give the playwrights exposure and the opportunity to see their piece with some rehearsal time. At this point, the drama-turgical development will typically be more about strengthening the choices that are there, looking to refine or clarify. If there are elements that seem to make the next step of full production more difficult, that will be a major source of conversation in this process. Finally, the play in production is a dramaturg's opportunity to help the playwright solidify the script and communicate with the production team. Close attention to process and a clear responsive point of view will help make any of these stages effective development.

Another thing that shapes and may complicate new-play dramaturgy is the impact of for whom the dramaturg is working. If she is the representative of the theatre or the festival, she will be working with the playwright with the goals of the producing body in mind. If she is freelancing and working with the playwright, the relationship may be affected by the potential complications of being a collaborator for hire. These are part of the circumstances of new-play dramaturgy, and do not have to be impediments to a good artistic partnership. Open and straightforward conversations and clarity of expectation and purpose will help to solidify the working relationship and create a more effective collaboration.

How do you like to work? This is a good way to start a relationship with a playwright and the first question that I like to ask when working with someone new. Establishing up front the expectations for the collaboration helps calm any fears the playwright may have about the influence of a dramaturg on his work, and also discussing a plan for communication and interaction keeps things open and clear. If the playwright prefers to see things in writing or likes to talk about character when he is drinking tea, these are ways to create an environment that can aid the process. In addition, asking the question delivers the message that the dramaturg is interested in working with the playwright, not at him. If the playwright does not have a preference or a specific idea, the dramaturg can offer suggestions or propose to try a particular mode and see how that goes. The collaboration is more effective when it is honest and straightforward, and the earlier the artists can arrive at that place the better. The less time spent wondering or quietly resenting the way things are going, the sooner the open and useful collaboration.

Chapter 4 looked at a variety of ways that timing is fundamental to the mindset to dramaturg. In the case of new-play dramaturgy, there is an important link to timing beyond that of when in the process to bring up certain issues. When one is a dramaturg on a new play, it is not only about this iteration of this script. When working with a playwright, the dramaturg is working on the development of a particular stage of a specific play, and more than that he is working with the development of a writer and a voice in the contemporary theatre. Consequently, when there are responses to comments or questions that do not make it into this play, they are not inconsequential. It is possible there are results of this collaboration that will come through in later works. So the dramaturg should take the collaboration to heart and treat it well; the possibility of making a real contribution to the theatre is in each conversation, in each room.

While the long-term project is affecting the voice of contemporary theatre, each project will have a short-term goal as well, which is where the process to dramaturg is useful. One of the things that will help the collaboration maintain focus is when there is a specific goal in mind. Is the play in early development to lead to a public reading and talkback? Is the dramaturg brought in by the theatre to help ensure the play is production ready? Was it selected for a new voices workshop production where part of the prize was time with the dramaturg to work through the piece? Is it a more informal arrangement, a playwright asked for some feedback? Each of these circumstances is a significant opportunity for new-play dramaturgy, and each requires its own approach determined by the goal of the collaboration.

The dramaturg has a clear purpose in mind, and this is one that she shares with the playwright. Ideally it is a purpose that has been determined in conjunction with the playwright's own goal for the interaction. Within the context of this purpose, she defines the project. The definition is further parsed from the overall goal. For example, if the purpose is to help ensure the play is production-ready for the theatre, the project may be to help the playwright condense the action into something more stageable than the version as is. If the dramaturg is working on a script for a development reading, maybe the project is to assist the playwright in a more complete character construction in order to discover what kind of audience response those characters inspire. The project may be to spend time with a playwright and his work and see what kind of overlap there is in terms of taste and style. The first phase of the process to dramaturg needs to support the larger goal; however, it still needs its own specific intent.

The content-gather is primarily the response to the text. This is an aspect that can be fraught and so really needs to derive from the definition and intent of the process. The most important aspect in this process is to remember that the point is the playwright's play. Every question, comment, and piece of material the dramaturg provides is in the service of the playwright's vision. The development process is about making it the best iteration of the play that the writer wants to write. This is a further example of the need to see clearly and engage with a work on its own terms rather than on any preconceived notion of what it should or could be. Also, depending on where things are in the process of the script, it could be too soon to discuss the substantive issues that could really unlock something and so the content-gathering would need to be limited to what is useful for that process. Every aspect of the mindset, facility with questions, seeing holistically, being attentive to timing and to the audience are useful in working with a playwright, and we as dramaturgs are most effective when we are able to apply that method with clarity and purpose.

Gathering the content for contextual input plays out differently as a new-play dramaturg. There are projects that require research in a traditional sense; however, this does not tend to be a large part of the job. Occasionally there are opportunities to assist the playwright in details of the ideas or issues they are attacking. Perhaps there are rituals that can be introduced, symptoms fleshed out, or travel routes navigated that can be brought in to support the trajectory of the text. Similarly the dramaturg may be able to bring in someone with expertise or firsthand knowledge to give additional context to a specific moment of the play or to its larger framework. Whether it is a specific experience – a character who lost a limb – or a general circumstance – a community decimated by a hurricane – the input that a dramaturg can offer to augment that of the playwright can be an effective aspect of new-play dramaturgy.

A new-play dramaturg can use their knowledge of theatrical process as well as understanding of script structure and dramatic analysis to assist. The dramaturg provides additional vocabulary to the discussion as well as a clear point of view on the technical strengths and weaknesses of the script. The dramaturg is familiar with the practical needs of the director, actors, and designers, as well as some artistic principles of script construction in order to have context for her own response to the work. The primary goal is to help the playwright bring her work to fruition, and part of what the dramaturg offers is her experience and a vision of what the work needs to be a play. Consequently, she tries to collaborate with the playwright to bring her vision to its most theatrically effective fruition, for the circumstances under which the collaboration occurs.

The final step, selecting the mode of communication, is primarily based on the agreement the dramaturg and playwright make about how to work. Type of project, style, and relationship will shape how the input is shared. If the collaboration is a short one, a couple of hours spent in conversation around a reading will not give much time or opportunity for a real in-depth discussion of theme and meaning. However, the dramaturg could facilitate a talkback structured around a specific question the playwright had about the script. This would be a way to contribute context and communicate a dramaturgical insight within the narrow parameters given.

A well-crafted talkback is the key to efficacy in new-play development. This can include specific questions the playwright presents, as well as the clarity of purpose on the part of the dramaturg. What is not useful is a talkback that turns into a group effort of rewriting the play; nor is the unrestrained commentary of an outspoken group. Talkbacks are often a point of conflict with playwrights, who may not see the value in the exercise. This response is usually the result of a bad experience and a circumstance where the discussion was not organized and was not useful. They are particularly challenging for young playwrights who may be just learning to find their own artistic voice as well as navigate the business of making plays.

In general a talkback that is conducted for the producing organization is intended to give the subscribers an opportunity to be heard. It is worth looking specifically at the new-play talkback in some more detail. It is a significant aspect of the development process and companies that are known for the development of new work often include talkbacks as part of that process. Perhaps the audience response will help a decision to offer a full production, or the response is part of the benefit the producer offers the playwright. The audience response, well moderated and from an articulate and well-informed theatregoing audience, can be a real asset to a playwright working on a new play. It can provide the writer with some insight into what the audience picked up on and how they responded to certain cues in the play. A post-show discussion can reveal what the audience was struck by, the questions they had and the overall impressions of the piece.

So what can the dramaturg do? She can approach the talkback with a clear purpose and be sure that the conversation stays on topic. She can contain the diversions and not allow the discussion to turn into suggestions for revisions. She can be the advocate for the play and the playwright, whether he is in the room or not, and ensure that they are both treated respectfully throughout the talkback. Some things to consider:

- Have a specific goal in mind; institutional, artistic, or community.
- Clarify with the playwright what questions she may like to have answered.
- Inform the audience of the purpose and rules of the talkback.
- Be sure the playwright is acknowledged in some way; remind the audience the artist is part of the conversation, whether she is in the room or not.
- Try to elicit brief, responsive comments from the audience. Encourage them to respond to what they saw, not what they expected.
- Maintain control of the conversation; redirect or stop conversations that start to try to make suggestions on the play.
- Remember this is public advocacy of the playwright and the institution.

As mentioned earlier, sometimes the dramaturg and playwright's collaboration is very short and related to a specific project or event rather than an entire production. When the collaboration is longer, it tends to be more in-depth with many opportunities for input and carefully crafted communication. This communication can take a number of forms; however, as discussed, using questions is an effective way to communicate with an artistic collaborator. Asking for clarification helps the playwright see the points on which she is clear and those that are still forming. The purpose of the interaction is to tease out the clearest and most effective construction of the play. If the dramaturg can bring into the discussion questions that help to continue the artistic exploration, in a well-conceived and direct manner, the playwright has more to work with in her process. Also, the dramaturg needs to be attuned to when it is no longer useful to bring more to the process. The holistic view will act as a reminder that while this interaction is contributing to the voice of the contemporary theatre, there is also a particular reading or production that needs to happen and specific needs to address. The dramaturg helps to make sure the process does not lose the forest for the trees.

Effective collaboration can be extraordinary and it is a goal worth striving for. Establishing a relationship and investing time and attention in the process of development helps to create the environment for that kind of exchange. When there is trust and connection, the dramaturg can be both a creative contributor and a strong advocate.

The saying that is resurrected for each generation of writers is "kill your darlings" and it is an important reminder that writers have to be able to cut their favorite bits or kill off something they love. It is good to remind the playwright that sometimes he has to cut good writing. The role of the dramaturg is not to tell him what writing to cut or what darlings to kill. The dramaturg can provide the context in which the playwright can discover that darling, and then hand him the mallet with which to kill it. The best input that a dramaturg can offer a play-wright is a clear, holistic response to the work they are given.

While the dramaturg may help the writer kill her darlings, at times she must also help to protect the ones that need to stay. This can be protection from the playwright, or from a director. One of the exciting things about working on new plays is the collaborative energy that can characterize that process, which can sometimes lead to a director making script suggestions to support her directorial role. For instance, if there is a scene that does not seem to be working, perhaps the direc-tor will suggest cutting the scene. This is a tricky negotiation because it may be that the scene is not working structurally and should be cut, or it may be that the director stopped looking for the staging solution.

The dramaturg can help shape the conversation, ask questions and offer varying perspectives for the collaborators to consider, and ultimately help defend the playwright's right to the play he wants to write.

The new-play dramaturg can end up providing a variety of services to the play; however, a fundamental aspect of his job is that the dramaturg is the advocate, sometimes for the playwright and sometimes for the play. These are different things and one of the challenges of effective dramaturging is to be able to recognize the difference and when to prioritize one over the other. Often the dramaturg is a liaison between the writer and the institution or between writer and director. In both of these circumstances the dramaturg may be called upon to act as a mediator in conflicts. She may find herself in a position where she needs to be an active advocate for the playwright if his point of view is being diminished. The understanding of the script and the goals of the production will help keep a clear point of view, and the mindfulness of communication techniques will hopefully serve the dramaturg well.

What do you do when the play is being diminished? The advocacy for the playwright is a more straightforward proposition than the advocacy for the play. The dramaturg has the person for whom she is taking up a cause, and has the validation that is what is warranted. When she is advocating for the play, sometimes it may be in opposition to the director and even the playwright. This is a more difficult argument since it seems to go in opposition to the desires of the playwright – particularly if that is what he claims. However, when the truth of the play is being challenged by a rewrite or a production choice, it is the responsibility of the dramaturg to be its defender. Ultimately it may be futile; it is the playwright's decision as it is the playwright's play. As a resource, the Dramatists Guild provides rules regarding these issues that are a good point of reference and reminder. At the same time, thinking in terms of contributing not just to a play but also to the body of work, it is a defense that may resonate later. Even if it does not, sometimes the dramaturg has to advocate for the play.

Play development is where a lot of dramaturgy is happening in the contemporary theatre, and a more connected mindset to dramaturg makes it more effective. There are a variety of models of play-making and its development, and a flexible, responsive dramaturgy can be at the forefront of that work. Good dramaturg-playwright collaboration is a strong contributor to the development of our theatre.

Devising

Devised theatre is an excellent kind of performance to dramaturg. The process-oriented form is itself a collaborative, holistic approach and process. Essentially, devising is dramaturging in some fundamental ways and so the two are well matched. Devising has been a mode of performance for a very long time, and is essentially an umbrella term for a kind of play that is generated through the process of rehearsal, and emerges in some fashion from that process. It is in the making of it that the script takes shape, and it is typically ensemble-generated and constructed. Devised theatre is created through the collaboration of artists in the room, so it is particularly well suited to dramaturgy.

The application of the mindset and process to dramaturg is the commonality of the various projects, and it is the flexible and responsive nature that allows for dramaturgy to be applied to so many different kinds of performance. An element that specifically distinguishes the dramaturgy for devised theatre from that of established script production or new plays is the function of the content the dramaturg provides. Rather than offering context to support the artistic choice made by the playwright, the dramaturg selects materials to provide a context that can prompt the artistic choice that will make it into the text.

Two main elements of devising that connect to dramaturgy are that it is an open, responsive collaboration and that it is constantly defining itself through its process. There are a number of different groups who work with devised theatre and each has its own purpose, goals, and practices. For example, work that is inspired by political activism may start with a topic and use devising techniques to explore the human cost of that issue. Another group may use devising to explore first-person accounts of a disaster and construct a narrative around them. An ensemble can work from movement-based performance inspired by visual imagery, or strong story-based works based on the retelling of classic tales. The common form is that the script of the performance is arrived at through the process of creation.

Devising relies on the just-in-time response of its collaborators and is malleable to fit the needs of the production and the audience. There is no established rule or encompassing definition of this mode of theatre-making; all of which sounds very much like the picture of dramaturgy, which also relies on the flexible thinking and creative response of its artists. As with dramaturgy, in devising the lines shift and the definitions are situation- and personnel-dependent. Both are defined by the purpose of the work, and who it is with/for.

Devised theatre is a dynamic artistic endeavor that stretches the artistic impulses of everyone involved. The presence of a dramaturg allows for the presence of an artistic collaborator who is invested in the meaning and outcome while enjoying a slight edge of outside perspective. Consequently, the dramaturg can be watching for the larger context of story structure and continuity, keeping track of the process benchmarks, and looking to the eventual presence of an audience, while the rest of the ensemble can stay immersed in the moment-to-moment work. In many ways the primary function of the dramaturg in devising is to be the champion of and advocate for the process.

What does it mean to be the advocate for the process? In the same way that the dramaturg will speak for the writer, the play, or the character, she stays committed to the method, perspective, and timing of the mode of play-making the ensemble exercises. Since the text for performance is a product of the rehearsal, the process of devising requires the ability to capture and shape that product. There may be a playwright as part of the ensemble, the writing may be shared among the group, or sometimes the dramaturg herself will take on the role of writer – either to pen or to transcribe what comes out of rehearsal. Regardless of how the text is generated, the dramaturg attends to its creation and helps to ensure that what results is a usable script for performance. Throughout the process of script construction, the dramaturg keeps sight of the larger context of the formation of a performance for an audience. Consequently, she makes sure the process is moving through the necessary stages to get to a text that can be performed and seen.

Another way the dramaturg acts as advocate for the process is to help the rest of the ensemble to trust the process. The dramaturg has the insider understanding of what the ensemble is striving for and the point of view of the audience's proxy and so can respond to the work with a clarity that helps reinforce the choices that may feel riskier to the ensemble. While the process of devising is exciting and can generate dynamic work, it can also be intimidating to work without the common material and seemingly stable foundation of an established text. The dramaturg can help an ensemble work through this uncertainty with her clarity of purpose and her input.

The devising process is different for any collection of artists. While there may be particular ways that individual directors or companies tend to work, specific physical and narrative activities they utilize, the outcome of these activities will be completely dependent on who is doing them. A project may consist of artists who are very effective physical improvisers and have a strong sense of ensemble connection through movement. Others may be specifically inspired by writing prompts that help to create a text-based foundation early in the process. Still others may find resonance in visual imagery and other kinds of composition. All of these are models that will shape a devised process and determine the manner in which the text for performance is constructed. This is part of the reason that devised theatre often comes from ensemble companies that continue to work together over time and develop a useful style of working. However, whether the ensemble is established or newly formed, the process of devising is shaped by those who are doing the work, and a flexible, responsive approach to the piece is absolutely vital. The mindset to dramaturg establishes the outlook with which to engage with the work on its own terms, without a specified agenda or bias.

Another aspect of the mindset that is applicable to devising is the ability to discover the questions to ask and those to answer. The dramaturg is a creative collaborator in a room set up for creative collaboration and since he has a slightly outside-the-process point of view as well, he can choose what questions should be brought in to spark conversation and which ones to answer to uncover significant moments in the story. All of the questions he would ask and answer from script and production team are brought into the process of devising in order to help guide the output into a coherent shape.

While timing is an important element in all dramaturgical work, it is of particular relevance in devising. The process that the dramaturg is sponsoring needs to have structural benchmarks and frequently the dramaturg will be watching the calendar as closely as she is watching the thematic construction. Understanding timing is in part a comprehension of the production schedule that reveals when certain kinds of questions or input are appropriate and useful. This is the case in devising as well, and attention to timing reminds the dramaturg to avoid talking about specific wording when the ensemble is working on the general story arc, and also allows her to usher the ensemble past the open discovery of story arc when it is time to lock down character and dialogue. Timing is additionally important as a dramaturgical tool for devising since it moves in both directions, knowing when it is useful to offer what input as well as recognizing at what point the targets need to be met. One way to advocate for the process is to ensure that the process of exploration ends with enough time to get into the mechanics of putting together a show.

The process is situation-dependent; consequently, the benchmarks will also depend on the project. However, there are some general guidelines to keep in mind. One of the challenges of devising is to recognize the points at which the explorations must give way to choices, and part of the process of dramaturging a devised piece is to help determine and adhere to those points. The process-driven work is dynamic and can lead to exciting revelations, and ultimately will be a performance for an audience. That is, assuming the piece is heading toward performance for an audience, of course, but whatever the goal, the process of getting there needs to keep in mind the forest and the trees. Consequently, there will be a point at which the story is determined, characters are crafted, and a plan for the performance is established. This point will happen with enough time to meet whatever rehearsal and technical needs are required. These markers will also reflect any showcases or events the piece may include. The process is an artistic exploration and also a practical composition of an event, and the dramaturg helps to ensure it is effective at both.

The artistic elements of devising are also necessarily flexible. An ensemble may include a playwright or composer, or members of the group may fill these roles. All of the company may perform or there can be facilitators and dramaturgs in addition to the performers. Again, whatever the combination, the dramaturg is looking holistically and making sure the process is effective. One significant contribution can be watching for the effectiveness of the devising, to see when the exploration stops being useful, when a storytelling exercise gets counterproductive or when a free-write is needed. Whether he is looking in or part of the performing ensemble, the dramaturg needs to see the whole and help the company move in the same direction.

Much of the work that is generated through devised techniques is issue-driven. Devising techniques are a widespread practice of social and political activist theatre and various kinds of agenda-based performance. Consequently, the dramaturg's active attention to the ideas and circumstances that connect an audience to a performance are particularly potent. In fact, devising enables the dramaturgy to construct this link in both directions. Rather than relying exclusively on linking the text of performance to an audience sensibility, the dramaturg can bring into the room the issues and rhetoric of the eventual audience and allow that to shape the performance itself. Devising allows for the questions of "Why this play? Why here? Why now?" to travel in both directions between audience and production in a dynamic and fundamental way.

The circumstances and events the community is confronting will be fodder for the ensemble. For example, if the inspiring topics deal with poverty and homelessness, then the material of the devising can include the stories, images, and places of those issues in that community. It is a "here, now" generative process and so can take inspiration from the immediate and the directly placed.

While the devising process itself is determined by the artists involved and the nature of the materials, the dramaturgical contributions are still dependent on how effectively they are defined. Each project has the opportunity to be enriched by the three steps to define, collect, and communicate the input, whatever that may be. For example, when working with an ensemble with issue-based material, such as homelessness, as the central focus, the dramaturg will be tasked with a number of different projects to support the process. He will identify ideas and perspectives from which to approach the subject matter. These tasks and perspectives are then given more specific form through the determination of end goal and target audience. Once that process of definition is complete, he can collect the materials to support it and determine the best mode of communication to his audience. This may be visual imagery and soundscape, or it could include bringing in people to speak of a personal experience. Or it can be any other point of contact that supports the needs of the piece and the goals of the performance. If the devised piece is working from an existing text, the dramaturg finds the relationship to that text by defining the project around it. For example, the intent could be to find a vocabulary in the text that can be used in the production. Word-association games or generated word clouds could be an effective way to explore the language used in the text.

The overall role of the dramaturg in the devised production, as well as each task he undertakes, will be framed and defined in a way to help support the technique of creation. The act of definition shapes each task to aid the process followed by the ensemble and continue the progress toward a performance. The process is further aided by the content that is gathered and compiled. This content will likely include many of the elements of production dramaturgy in terms of well-researched and synthesized materials about context. However, this aspect of the dramaturg's output can work in a slightly different way than in a scripted production. As mentioned earlier, the dramaturg's materials are meant to give an impetus to the creation of the text rather than to provide context for it. The materials are not the casebook of words, ideas, and images that flesh out the skeleton of the script in order to transition to the stage; they are themselves the materials that generate the text of the production.

The final step, the selection of mode of communication, is as much about the ensemble as it is about the material. The dramaturg is in the room in devised theatre and so he knows how the ensemble most effectively generates material. That knowledge will inform how the content will be communicated. If the ensemble is visual or tactile, more story-based or particularly connected to music, the dramaturg can find the mode of presentation that effectively shares the content he has collected. In devising, it is particularly important that the material is in the room; consequently, the dramaturgical output is often more reliant on tangible artifact than digital communication. The established connection to the ensemble and its method of devising establishes the foundation on which to generate and communicate the dramaturgical input.

In rehearsal, the dramaturg and director will institute a way of working, as is the case in the other collaborations discussed. Open communication and clear expectations are always going to improve the process and the relationship. Devising as a model tends to allow for a greater sense of the collaboration and often has a "go with the best idea in the room" nature. That will often result in the dramaturg being a more vocal presence and will tend to see less of the formality of all questions or comments going through the director. However, there is structure and there are parameters to the nature of the collaboration and the dramaturg needs to be conscious of those practiced and nuanced shifts. In general, it is still a useful policy to establish with the director the kinds of dramaturgical input and the ways of incorporating them in the context of the rehearsal space. The protocol of rehearsal and the understanding of the ensemble need to be respected, and the mindfulness with which input and response are offered is as complete in devised theatre as it is in any other model.

> TIP: *Create an environment for creativity with what you bring to the room.*

Traditional research materials, experts in a field, artistic or thematic objects, shared experiences, exercises, stories, challenges to the work; the dramaturg's contribution can take many forms. In devised theatre, that input is particularly significant because it is part of the process that shapes the very text of the performance. It is a role that is dynamically redefining itself within a process that is doing the same. The flexible thinking, holistic viewpoint and responsiveness are well suited to the dynamic nature of the work. The clarity of purpose, attention to timing, and the close link to audience are vital to keeping the process nimble and effective.

Devising is a kind of performance in which everyone is practicing dramaturgy by virtue of devising the piece.

Dramaturgy is an inherent aspect of devised theatre. The devising process itself is aided by the inclusion of an ensemble member who is there specifically to dramaturg. Playwriting is also inherently dramaturgical. A new play benefits from the contributions of an informed creative collaborator who is invested in the playwright's creation. Neither of these models is reliant on the presence of a dramaturg to exist, just as an established script production can run without a dramaturg. Yet they all can be better, be more fully realized, have a greater connection to the audience, and have deeper resonance for the performers when they are effectively dramaturged. This activity, the process to dramaturg, is the science to make the production more.

Exercises

These exercises are intended to be a starting point to help define the kind of role and relationship the dramaturg has to new and not-yet-scripted work.

Practice Reading

The purpose is to get you into the mindset of a script reader and have the opportunity to practice reading with purpose and correspondence with playwrights.

1. Read a series of ten-minute plays and write readers' reports. Practice what you are looking for when you read a new work and how to capture that in a shareable short form.
2. Decide on a contest or season for which to read. Use another series of short plays to practice making the selection based on performance criteria.
3. Craft letters to playwrights, rejecting or accepting the work, and/ or asking for further material.

Devised Work

To help think about process in devising.

1. Using an existing text, map out the process to devise a work based on that text.
2. Using a series of images, map out a process to devise a work based on the images.
3. Create a schedule of benchmarks from initial meeting to production for a devised piece.

10

NOTES FROM THE FIELD

Up to this point we have considered ways to develop a point of view and to practice a method that will help to make the dramaturg a more effective artistic collaborator. We have examined dramaturg as a verb, as a way to curate an experience for an audience. This way of seeing helps to create a point of view for the dramaturg that is flexible and holistic, and helps to develop a process that is attentive and responsive. The notion of dramaturg as verb is an effective way to approach the role and the process can help the tasks of the dramaturg.

The opportunity to share stories is a primary path to understanding what is possible as a dramaturg. One of the benefits of professional organizations like Literary Managers and Dramaturgs of the Americas (LMDA) and other opportunities to gather dramaturgs together is the chance to trade ideas and stories. These opportunities to share discoveries and best practices can be incredibly helpful in honing the craft. Sometimes the most useful are the anecdotes of dramaturgical "wins," the projects and moments in which a solid artistic collaboration occurs. These stories serve as a good reminder of what dramaturgy can be, and provide a way to expand our understanding of what it means to dramaturg.

The purpose of this chapter is to offer a similar kind of experience, to share stories about when it works and offer ideas about the skills and practices that help develop dramaturgy and dramaturgs. These stories give a sample of the kinds of things that professional and student dramaturgs are doing in the field and some of the things that they have learned along the way. For continuity, they will be talked about in the first person, although they are from multiple sources and multiple places. Also, the plays and theatres have been deliberately left out; this is not intended to connect to a specific work but to inspire thinking about different ways to approach dramaturgical work.

The chapter is separated into sections and starts with a couple of examples of the ways that dramaturgs define the craft. Next there is a discussion about working on productions, including working with directors and actors. Then we will look at some ideas about new plays and devised projects, and then some advice for early-career dramaturgs. Finally, the chapter concludes with some best practices and tips intended to help you develop as a dramaturg. Again, the idea is not a comprehensive guide, but a way to think about dramaturgy. It is a way of seeing and engaging with material and audiences. That is a perspective that continues to develop and expand in our theatre and is a way of ensuring our role as a creative collaborator in play-making of any kind.

Metaphors for Dramaturgy and What Do You Do?

One of the recurrent themes of the story exchange among dramaturgs is the ongoing use of metaphor. It is a go to when asked to explain what one does for a living, be it from family members or people on airplanes. In addition, the metaphor can be useful when explaining what we can offer to a potential employer. There are a number of reasons we resort to analogy when discussing the work, one of which is that it is a difficult job to describe it in general, and then it changes from project to project. In addition, the notion of dramaturgy as a way of seeing and engaging resists limited and fixed definition and relies on other ways to explore this dynamic and elusive perspective. As discussed at the beginning of the book, the metaphor is just a stand-in; however, it can sometimes offer insight into the more substantial question for those working in the field – what can dramaturgy do?

When it works, dramaturgy can be a well-integrated collaborative tool. In describing a tool, metaphors become useful and can perhaps help to shape our understanding of the activity. There are a number of metaphors and analogies that are used to describe the role and they provide insight into how dramaturgs see their work.

Navigational images are useful, the dramaturg becoming the guide who moves the production in the right direction. Similarly, some see the dramaturg as cartographer, shaping the path more than steering it.

Scientific images work as well – the notion of the kind of questioning and examining that the dramaturg does through each step of the process of creation, evaluating, and testing his hypotheses throughout the process. There are a number of analogies around the idea of creating or constructing – creative if not generative. These include architectural images of compiling the materials assembled, or cooking images that indicate the role as one that ensures a right combination in order to make the end product.

The more dynamic metaphors seem to be most effective. To add another one to the mix, the dramaturg functions as a conduit – she amps up the connections between script and production, between production and spectator, between experience and audience. Sometimes the notion of dramaturg as translator or intermediary clouds the impression and implies that she is somehow in between the other collaborators, acting as an intermediary that may hamper the connection. The electrical analogy fixes this by recognizing that the dramaturg on a project can increase the amplitude of the connections. The production does not (should not) need an intermediary standing between content and audience, but a conduit that strengthens the relationships can be a very useful thing.

We as dramaturgs work with images, and sometimes we talk about our work through the lens of what we do, though even that needs to be framed in the more theoretical. Once again, dramaturgy is not a collection of tasks, but a way of working. That way of working can be characterized in different ways. The dramaturg is someone who is equally comfortable in the rehearsal room and the library. The dramaturg is provider of the context. He is the keeper of the story, witness, story detective, historical advisor, structural engineer, mechanic, or surrogate.

Another way we talk about what we do is through the use of active verbs. These are probably some of the most useful ways to think about what it means to dramaturg. Among the verbs that dramaturgs use to define their role: listen, question, excavate, connect, explore, bridge, advocate, support, synthesize, articulate, advise, curate, and contextualize.

Dramaturging Productions

The process of dramaturgy depends on the play, the production, and the personnel. The nature of the process is determined by the amount of time available to dedicate to that work. The more time spent with a collaborator, the greater the trust built and the more expanded the opportunities to sync style and perspective. Many of the formalities can be done away with once you have a working style and relationship that is effective for a process. However, it does not have to take until the third project to have a genuine artistic collaboration. As discussed earlier, open communication and clear expectations are a way to get off to a strong start, and the continued practice of the holistic viewpoint, flexible thinking, and close attention to timing and purpose will add to the likelihood of a useful working relationship.

It comes down to working with people, and that is the most important part of being a dramaturg, navigating the relationships in a way that lets you do the work and contribute to the production. Sometimes that means weathering a more contentious relationship. One of my favorite stories is one that Mark Bly tells. He was working on a production of Ibsen's *Hedda Gabler* and was having a conversation with the director outside the rehearsal. The director was taking issue with the action of the play and flat out said, "People just don't do that." To which Mark replied, "Hedda Gabler f★★★ing does." This is an example of those times the dramaturg is advocate for the playwright, and also gives the reminder that although the view is holistic and not limited to one production element, the dramaturg is invested.

Working with Directors

The working relationship with directors is one of the primary indications of effective dramaturgy. The production model in most cases has the director in charge of the production, and the director generally vets the materials, information, and communication with actors and designers. Sometimes this will mean all comments and questions go to her and then are disseminated by her, and other times it will simply mean the agreement is clear about what is given directly to a member of the production team and when. The initial meetings with the director will hopefully clarify these expectations and again, the more time spent working with a director, the clearer those lines become.

An effective collaboration means the work gets done, not that it is without conflict. Depending on the styles and personalities of the artists involved, the effective artistic union can be full of argument, as long as that is what is useful to everyone involved. I had a director with whom most of my interactions were arguments about the meaning of things, but it really made us both get very specific and clear in our opinions and I think made the work we both did much better.

One of my more challenging relationships was more about the director's concern about his own authority, I think. This director would pretty much shut down anything I said in rehearsal or in production meetings. He was vocal about his discomfort with dramaturgs. But every night he would call me after rehearsal and we would talk for a half an hour and go over what had happened that night. He just could not let that happen in front of the production team; it would be admitting something, maybe? So I could do my job; it just had to be on the phone outside rehearsal.

On the other hand, working with a director once you have already formed a relationship can be really fulfilling and comfortable. There is one director, we work together a lot and we have built a lot of trust so I can just give notes or ask questions directly to the actors. It is a very open rehearsal process so there is never the need to check with the director to make sure this is all right. Of course this was after a relationship was already built and we knew our styles and our points of view were aligned. It feels like such a time save and I can gear my comments directly to the actor rather than feeling that they need to convince the director as well as be meaningful to the actor.

One of the best relationships I had was when the director and I always sat together and we quickly got to a place where I could just reach over and write a note on his notepad, and vice versa. It wasn't so much a concern about whether to give the note to the actor or not, but when the director wanted to handle the points raised, and if it was something that he or I would take up. It was a great way to work and we both really felt the collaborative nature of the whole process.

It can also happen that the relationship between dramaturg and director is borderline hostile, which tends to be less useful. Even when the relationship is just uncertain, it can feel as if a lot of time is wasted trying to navigate that, and occasionally you are in a situation with a person and you just cannot make it work. Some directors are suspicious of dramaturgs, and other members of the cast and crew may not see value in the presence of another artistic point of view. It is often a misguided understanding of the role that leads to this skepticism – I had a director who told me he did not like to work with dramaturgs because he preferred to do his own research. Unfortunately, this is not an uncommon reaction from directors; however, this perspective can be dealt with when you work with a creative team and have the opportunity to show them what dramaturgy can be. Dramaturgical output is not doing someone else's research, it is an insider's knowledge and understanding but with a kind of critical objectivity of an outsider. The artistic input you can bring means you are able to ask the right questions or say something new or in a different enough way that it can open up a moment or a character or a play. Being in the room and knowing what the director wants gives you a special and valuable perspective. One of the best things about the perspective you bring is that you do not have to figure out how to make it work, you just get to see how it is working.

When the relationship is adversarial from the onset, this may end up stalling your chances of being integrated into the production process. If the director does not want you talking to actors and does not want to hear what you have to say, there is not a whole lot that you can do. It is possible that you can change their mind, and there may be things you can do to improve the situation, depending on why they are opposed.

Sometimes you run into a director who is worried about the dramaturg as a challenge to their authority and this can be a hard thing to work around. Occasionally it can be taken care of by frank conversations about the process and establishing clear boundaries and expectations. Once the collaborators get to know each other a little better, the suspicion can lessen, or you just work in a way that maintains very clear lines of authority. Even when things stay a little uncertain, you can frequently find something to add, whether the focus is more on audience outreach or working with the designers.

A director may have had a bad experience with a dramaturg and this shapes their attitude toward the role. This situation can be more difficult to combat because it often results in active resistance so as not to repeat a previous incident. The impulse is to push back. Just because there was a bad experience does not mean the role should be discounted – that is not the case when you have a bad time with an actor. However, the analogy does not work; productions can and do happen without a designated dramaturg. The purpose is to remind or show the people you are working with why the production is better with one.

One of the real challenges to the dramaturg is that in some settings you are called upon to defend or justify your place in the room. To address this, the dramaturg needs to find a way to reframe that demand and clarify his autonomous role, while at the same time give himself license to actively occupy his place in the room. Understanding the role as creative collaborator and practicing methods that help your contribution to be effective and vital are the most expedient ways to inhabit that space. Even when the rest of the people at the table are not totally welcoming, it is good to remember that you have something special to offer.

The need to defend is intensified when working with collaborators who are mistrustful or downright hostile to the role of dramaturg. While there are tactics that may mitigate this situation or things that can be done despite the resistance, sometimes the gap is too large. This may be the only time you work with that collaborator and it is good to remember that while the collaborative action may often be instigated by the dramaturg, it is not his responsibility to carry it all. It is not a one-direction proposition or relationship, and if there is not the opportunity for artistic collaboration, it is not a place you want to dramaturg.

Dramaturgy in Practice

The relationship gives you access to the collaborators, which is important in terms of being able to offer content and input. The other important element of that is actually being in the room. Some dramaturgs prefer to come and go in rehearsal; they are very present in the early rehearsal and then want to be able to come in for run-throughs with relatively fresh eyes in order to be more effective at being the surrogate audience. There can be a lot of value in seeing a run-through that you have not watched being assembled piece by piece. It allows for a point of view that mimics the eventual theatrical audience's experience more closely. To that end, it can be an effective way to explore questions of continuity and structure. That intent may supersede the desire to be in the rehearsal. Other dramaturgs attend as many rehearsals as possible because missing rehearsals means you are not in the room to see where things are going, to build on what happens, to address questions as they arise. Ultimately it is up to the dramaturg, her collaborators, and the needs of the production when she is in rehearsal. Be sure to have a clear purpose that determines when you are in the room, and when you are not.

Good things can happen when you are in the room, and it is through being there that you learn what is needed. Sometimes the work you do leads up to a specific moment. One of my best moments in a production was during tech when the director had a question about the use of a scrim to create the distinction between indoor and outdoor scenes. There was a technical impetus to the choice, and when we talked about it my opinion was based on how the use affected the story and connected it to some other things in the play. It is funny when you have one of those moments and you realize it is not about the quality of notes or the different things you give the director. That whole process came down to that one moment in tech. I was there, ready for that question.

The revelations that do not necessarily show in reading the script may show themselves only when you see them playing out. I was working on a production and was sitting in rehearsal listening to a character go through the list of names of those who had come before and I was struck by what was happening – it was a kind of litany of saints. As many times as I had read through and talked about the play, I had never gotten this impression, but after hearing it spoken, it was evident that is what was happening. I leaned over to the director and said, "This is his litany; it is what reminds him he is not alone." It ended up being a huge breakthrough for the character and the play.

Those moments of revelation during rehearsal are great, and it is exciting to be able to share them with the director and actors. On another show I worked on, there is a character who is unable to speak, he can't communicate, and then there is a very emotional scene where he tests a speech-generating device and he types, "I love you." It was an action that was intended to disturb his wife and then the scene would continue, but there was something that just did not feel right. One night I was watching the scene and I leaned over to the director and said, "I don't think that's about him, I think that's about her mother." The director gave that note to the actors and it really helped shape the scene immediately. A couple of weeks later the actor who played the wife told me that moment also really helped her to unlock something significant for the character.

It is exciting when you get to see your work artistically inform the production. I worked on a show about a wrestler. To prepare, I watched hours and hours of wrestling and got a deep sense of the physicality, how wrestlers used the space as well as the signature moves of some of the characters. When there were problems blocking scenes I was able to bring in how wrestlers used the space to inform the blocking so that work was directly connected to the staging of the show. Also the actors then incorporated specific signature moves that were based on real wrestlers so they were an "Easter egg" situation for audience members who knew wrestling. It was a strange kind of research, but it ended up being a physical context that was really important to the production.

As a dramaturg, there are so many different ways you can find to artistically inform the production. For instance, I often find myself contributing music suggestions for scene changes or curtain calls. The things you find, the pieces you bring in to help create the context for the company, have a funny way of finding themselves on stage. I worked with the actors to create playlists for their characters in a show and we brought them into rehearsals to play during breaks and then started incorporating the ones that became the kind of signature songs into the warm-ups. By the time we got to tech, these songs had been co-opted and were used for all of the scene changes and seemed to make the whole production more connected to the characters.

The ways we work in the rehearsal change from project to project and I find that one thing that is consistent is the fact that you are there as witness. This realization helps to inform the dramaturgy in a lot of ways, and it is incredible how often just allowing yourself to be a witness is what the show needs more than anything else. I worked on a show with a director I had worked with before. We had a really good working relationship but were having a little problem communicating on this one. In rehearsal, the end of the first act was just not working. I had talked with the director a couple of times and asked questions about intent and meaning, but he was just not seeing a way to solve the problem. It was starting to be a real problem because the moment did not make a lot of sense and it caused a real stumble in the tempo of the piece. One night during a break I just described the scene to him, told him what I saw sitting in the audience. I talked through the act, beat by beat, this happens and then this happens, and he just stared at me for a moment. Then he said, "That's not right." We went back in and he reblocked the scene completely. I did not need to tell him anything other than what I witnessed.

The idea of witness is important. You are witness to what is happening in the moment but also to what has happened already. One of the big things a dramaturg offers is the knowledge of the original intentions. For example, I worked with a company that was really committed to the politics of the piece we were doing. There were a couple of points over the course of the production where I felt the play was kind of losing its way and so I brought in some materials about the political issue to get people back into the mindset of why they were doing this work. I did not have to say anything about the various ways the production was or was not effective political theatre; I just needed to remind them of what they were doing.

There are also times when you are really there to witness – to watch what is happening. During a tech run I was in charge of watching for nuances and physical details while the director fine-tuned the bigger-stage picture. During a scene on a fire escape in the bitter winter, I noticed something off – where was the winter cold? The characters touched the metal railings with their bare hands without any kind of physical reaction. They conveyed "cold" only with their hunched torsos. I mentioned it to the director during a break, cluing him into the neglected tangible experiences, and he also noticed their absence and gave the note to the actors. Sure enough, when the actors modified their reactions in accordance with their surroundings, it made the decision to risk the cold rather than stay inside much more effective and enhanced the contrast between that scene and the following one that was set during the warm and sunny spring.

The content you provide for the production team with your case-book and presentations is really important and useful to the process, you hope, and even still I find most of my best moments are things that happen in the moment in rehearsal. There was a play that has several dreams in it and actually ends on a dream. We were having trouble with it because the end was just not effective during tech; it just felt as if we were not ending it. We were watching the dream figures come through the front door and I said, "You know, when I dream things aren't in the right place." For the director it was an incredible "oh yeah" moment and she changed the blocking of the scene. On the next run-through the new blocking made all the difference and completely solved the issue. From this offhand comment, "You know, when I dream . . ."

Working with Actors

Some of the greatest moments in a rehearsal process are the ones that unlock a character for an actor. Whether it is an idea or an image that you bring to them or the right question at the right time, so much of your work goes to the actor and it is exciting to see how they use it. Sometimes you bring in things for them to look at or do – for one show I taught an actor how to play Russian solitaire, and for another one brought in soda bread for everyone to taste. Teaching Russian solitaire was actually so she could play it onstage, but the soda bread was a part of a kind of cultural immersion moment. The play was about an Irish Catholic family who were very devout. None of the actors were Catholic so we had "Catholic Day" and brought in icons and showed the daily rituals of Catholicism so they could not only ask questions but also handle the physical objects and get a sense of the personal practice of the religion. I try to do those kinds of things when I can. These types of experiences are a good way to bond as a company, and it is more significant because you are bonding around or within the world of the play.

Dramaturgy is making connections between the material and the needs of the actor. It is about making sure that your work and output are present in the room, and informing the shape of the production, not merely collating facts. When you find ways to bring a creative point of view into the room and into the process, not in terms of injecting it, but joining the process, that is when the dramaturgy can be most effective for the actor. You can do it in the way you help them work with the language, with the objects and ideas you bring in, and just by being in the room. You know the play, so it is a great vantage point from which to help an actor develop a character.

I got to work on a show that was true collaboration in the real sense of the word. The director had a clear vision and was open to input so I was able to really contribute to the conversations. I worked a lot with the cast and set up movie nights so they could see some work from the period. I circled places mentioned in the script on an old map and we used that a lot, and I brought in a small library of books to rehearsal that we could talk about in breaks and which the actors could borrow. We talked about what kinds of drugs the characters used and their effects and came up with as many ways as possible to explore the world the characters inhabited. The production had characters on stage the whole time, so all of this helped the in-between moments in the play.

I discovered there was so much more sustenance when the actor does the work in collaboration with the dramaturg.

Collaborating with actors is a big part of what I do as a dramaturg and I am always trying to find different ways in for character work. Usually the most effective things are the ones that happen outside rehearsal. One time this worked really well was when the company got together every morning for the week of tech rehearsals and the run of the show at 4:48 am and we just sat together and listened. It was a tough show and everyone was pretty raw by the time it went into tech, and I can't really tell you why that worked, but there was something about us all being together, just being together. Not doing anything, just fifteen minutes a morning of being in the moment. It was a company bonding thing but it also really brought them into the place of the play. That kind of work can be really useful, as long as you are working with people who are willing to jump in like that. And as a dramaturg, sometimes you just have to take those kinds of chances, too. There was one production where the characters had a daughter who had died. During the process it became apparent that much of the play was defined by the girl's absence, so I wanted to create a presence for her so they could feel the absence. I basically wrote myself into the play and I wrote two reports as the daughter, and I made a family tree. The kind of things parents would have kept from her childhood. It was possibly the most intrusive I have ever been but possibly the most meaningful work with actors I have done.

A dramaturg takes chances, sometimes with the actors in rehearsal and sometimes with the community she is representing. Sometimes it is just a matter of trying something to see if it will work. I worked on a play where the reveal at the end was that the story was a lie and so I had two lobby displays. When the audience came in, I did a magazine version with the story and then after the show they came out to newspaper headlines – was it a lie or not? I wasn't sure if the audience would bother to read things on the way out or not, but sometimes you don't know if it's going to work but you just have to do it to see. This was a company that was really trying to work on audience engagement so I thought that any chance we could connect with them again was worth trying. The key is to be willing to try things that are not proven yet, to take a risk that something may fall flat, but that is the only way you can find something new that does work. I worked with a director who said that to her actors – "I don't know, try something." I think that works as good advice for artists in general.

There has to be an environment that allows the kind of in-depth collaboration you can have as a dramaturg, and that is either part of the culture of the place or something that you have to really work to establish. Once you have it, there is so much you can offer to the process. We were doing a production where the characters were teenage boys in a boarding school. I gave the actors homework, to build connection to the lives the boys lived – they had to do reports on poets that were mentioned in the script. It helped give the actors a sense of who these boys were, and it became an important part of the ensemble work. That work came out of an environment that had the time and collaboration where you could say something and someone runs with it. That idea had actually come up before; we were reading the script and talking about it a month before rehearsals started and someone said we should give them homework assignments. So I did and it ended up being a key to that production. It's the same way we came up with the idea of a Hall of Fame of Women Scientists. We asked why we did not know more names and said that there should be cards, like baseball cards. So we made some. It is the kind of company that really relishes the time the artists can spend together talking through ideas and even better, actually following through with the ideas.

The model environment for a dramaturg is one that is completely committed to collaborative art. It's ideal when it is in that organic place: total collaboration, no ego, just a sense of "let's everyone bring their best self to the table." It's great for ethos. It is an ethos that can be extended into the audience interaction as well. One of the great things about my job is the audience engagement, especially when there is tricky subject matter. We bring in partners as part of community engagement; I reached out to all those people with an intersection work or interest in the piece. Then I had a curated conversation series with the audience as well as with the cast in rehearsal. It really deeply informed the actors and deepened the contextual understanding for the audience. The guests were part of the whole process, so that made it really exciting. There was a really strong sense of us all being part of something, company and audience.

The most rewarding kind of work is when you feel you did something that directly affected the production. It does not have to be something huge, and much of the time it is a small thing that you take away as the "win." I found this an interesting way to explain something that had to be explained. Sometimes it really is as simple as that. But that's important. A lot of the time we seem to deal with the minutiae, but it is really the details that we are watching, and you should not underestimate the details. I have a designer friend who says that the quality of a set design is found in the seams, that it is the level of detail and the invisibility of the transitions between one scenic element or material and another that is the real tell about the quality of the work. That works as a construction image, and also in play structure. Think about how many plays are made or broken by their transitions. The point is that the specificity of the details are important to make the piece more immediate, more connected, more real. Having someone who can look with details in mind, and know what they are looking at and for, is only going to help the production. There was a play we were doing that took place in the late nineteenth century and there was a sequence where they had to use an old camera. I had to keep reminding the actors to hold still and that they couldn't blink for a really long time. It takes a long time and the photographer would stop you if he caught you messing around. Once they got that, it was so much more interesting an event. It wasn't just that it was more accurate; it was a completely different moment full of energy and tension.

The kinds of things that you end up needing to learn about through production work tend to be pretty eclectic, and the running joke for some of the truly bizarre things with which you gain some expertise is, "I'm a dramaturg." It is useful, though. The more information you collect, the more you can draw from when you are working on something, and it is surprising how much overlap you find among different subjects. When there is something that is unfamiliar, then it is usually your job to figure it out and be able to explain it to the company. Maybe it is how you assemble a box on an assembly line, or how different drug paraphernalia is used. There was one time that I had to explain corporate structure to a cast. Another time there was a lot that happened because of the volatility of the stock market. I gave them a spreadsheet with the changing values of their stocks with each switch so they knew at each line exactly how much it would cost them. It was the kind of the thing that the playwright structured deliberately and once the actors had a stronger sense of what the characters would have understood, it was just better. The audience did not need to know the amounts; they would know when it really mattered to the characters.

Finding context is expected from the dramaturg, but it is more than offering a collection of facts. The things that I learn and the information I bring to my actors are always for a reason, something that they can work with to do their job. Even the most direct entries in the glossary are there for a reason. I will include a location that is mentioned because it may be that is where your character walked from that morning, and you probably want to know that it was six miles away. One time I built an online interactive map so that people could do a guided tour through the real and imaginary places mentioned in the play. I did not make it just because it was a neat thing – although it was – but because it gave the company something they could use to help them make this production.

Working with New Plays and Devised Projects

In the previous chapter we discussed how new-play dramaturgy and devising have their own attributes; however, they work from the same foundation in dramaturgical mindset and process. The successes derive from the same places as well: effective collaboration, open communication, attention to the needs of the production.

Working with a playwright is the best part of my job, and when you have worked with someone for a while and start to have the common language of earlier plays and even other ideas, it can be an incredibly creative partnership. I read his plays and ask questions and do all the new-play dramaturgy things, but sometimes I think the most important part of my job is to give him a chance to say things out loud. He talks through questions, characters, ideas, and problems and I swear he works out ninety percent of it before he actually types a word. The more we work together the better I am at being an active sounding board.

The kind of work we do with new plays varies depending on the circumstances. There have been times when I read a script with specific questions from the playwright: Does the character development seem organic? Does the end make sense? And that was the extent of the work I did on that project. Other times I was there while the playwright took it all apart and put it back together again. You just have to pay attention and be what the play and the playwright need at that

moment. There was a piece I worked on, it had been a blog that was
shaped into a play and I worked on the very early script development
and then later on with the full production. In the original form there
was a museum metaphor that was really interesting but by the time it
came into rehearsal it was not foreground enough to even be recognizable. It was the thing that tied it into the initial blog and really had
been a connecting piece and so I worked with the writer to bring it
back in. It ended up being a part of the set and the lobby display, and
we ended up creating a whole motif to support the work. Since I knew
it had been there at the start, it was a matter of reminding the writer.

There are also those times when you are the point of negotiation
between playwright and director, or are a line of defense for the audience. When the subject matter is particularly difficult, or the treatment
of it is problematic, you need to help find a way to something that
is workable for everyone. In the second act of a gory new musical,
a playwright was firm that a pair of teenaged characters trapped in a
high school should be handed guns by their captor and either shoot
each other or be shot by their captor. The director was struggling with
this literal stage direction, especially dealing with a shooting in a high-
school setting. The director suggested changing the text so that the
captor shot them but in the abstract and the deaths were offstage. The
playwright insisted that the captor be the one to shoot the teenagers
and that they die onstage. The crux rested in finding a solution that
implied onstage shooting and death with less visceral violence. The
playwright, director, assistant director, and I discussed this dilemma
throughout an extended lunch break and came to a compromise: the
guns were mimed using exaggerated choreography and hand gestures,
and the deaths occurred onstage. The playwright was pleased that
her conception of the moment stood and the director was pleased to
achieve high stakes with less gore.

Sometimes you just need to be able to support the choices the playwright has to make by being there to talk through them. Often the
work on play development is helping to navigate between a director
who is trying to get the play onto its feet and a playwright who is trying to tell the story he wants to tell.

As mentioned earlier, devising is a practical dramaturgy and the creation of the piece is well suited to — and requires — a dramaturgical point
of view. This means that one of the best things about those projects is

that you do not have to argue for your place in the room. The thing to do in that work then is to find where you can be the most useful, and do that. I worked on a piece once where my main point of contact was with the director. There were things I brought to the ensemble and I worked with the performers in some capacities, but mostly I worked through the day-to-day plan with the director and helped him stay on schedule and on topic. The notes I had for actors or story went through him, outside of the rehearsal process, and the majority of the questions I answered and input I gave went directly to him.

Best Practices and Advice to Early-Career Dramaturgs

The best advice I can offer is in terms of how to work as a dramaturg. It is said a lot but it can be said more. The most effective way to go about giving feedback is to ask questions. Describe what you see and then ask if that was intended. Ask what they are going for. Ask as many questions as you can to keep the conversation moving so the production staff are talking about the things they need to. Ask for clarification and ask to point out things that maybe the rest of the company are not seeing clearly. Questions are the most effective way to get information, and they are a great way to point out gaps in someone's understanding by making them say it out loud.

Another piece of practical advice that is always good to remember is to be someone people want to work with. This sounds obvious, and I hope that it is; however, some people seem to forget it. Even if you are doing a job you are not interested in, or working on a show that you hate, the people around you are people who can potentially get you the next job. And we want to work with good people who want to be there. It is hard enough to do a show; you do not want to do it with someone who makes it harder.

See theatre. As much as you can: new plays, revivals, whatever is happening in your city. See what people are doing, the things that are new, things that feel dated. Notice reactions from the audience, and your own reactions. Watch theatre, read plays, spend as much time as you can and immerse yourself in other people's art, too. When you see work that you really like, that inspires you, go and meet the people who made it. If you are looking to break into a city as a freelancer, a good place to start is by going to the people who are doing the kind of work you want to do. Who is doing the kind of work you are interested in? Do they have dramaturgs? What kind of lobby display and outreach are they offering? Is that something you can offer? But you start by knowing what kind of art inspires you. That is not to say that you will always be working on that kind of thing, but you should know what it is, and you should aspire to see as much of it as possible and work on it as much as you can.

Advice for an early-career dramaturg is a challenge because there are so many different paths to get there. There are some who get MFAs in dramaturgy, some who go via internships, some who shift from another creative role in the theatre and some who come in via other fields entirely. There is not a single, or even a best path. It is worthwhile to look at the resume of people who have the jobs that you want, though even with that you need to remember that the industry changes, so do not model your path based on what was effective for someone ten years ago. Even those who come from other areas in the theatre argue about what is the best training for a dramaturg. Some claim acting is the ideal preparation, since you know what an actor needs from a script. Others claim it is directing, since you can look big picture. A lot of dramaturgs are also playwrights, and designers understand composition better than anyone, so that would seem like a good option, too. Once again, the takeaway is that there is not a path laid out, so you will need to be open to the possibilities, you will need to dramaturg your career. I feel that most of the work I have done, I didn't learn in school. You can't learn it except by doing it. You learn how to grow in the field and develop your own personal aesthetic and discover what you're interested in. You need the chance to dig in and figure out what speaks to you.

One of the ways to navigate the early career, and the not-so-early career, is to look at the skills you have. Dramaturgy gives you a skillset that includes research, writing, and communication. It's a toolbox for working in the theatre or beyond. Dramaturgs are filling a lot of positions in education and community engagement. The challenge is to use that skillset for something that's marketable and paid work, together with all those other things you know and can learn how to apply. I think it comes down to one main thing: finding a building block of what you want to do.

It is also worth remembering that it is not an easy career to find. You have useful skills but you need to have your eyes open about the jobs and be open to the experiences you have and where they take you. Put yourself out there with a strong sense of "this is what I want, this is what I can do." Those things take energy and you spend a lot of your time looking for the next job. There are very few paid gigs, so you have to hustle. Also, remember that it can be really tiring, so it's OK to take a break and then get back to the hustle.

Recognizing that it is going to be difficult, like any job in the arts, and that there is not a roadmap that you can take is an important part of the process. That allows you to accept the fact and then get to work. Once you do that, you have to find the balance between the art that sustains you and the work that keeps you afloat. There is no path clarity; you have to figure out for yourself a quality of life and how long you are willing to pursue it. No one makes those decisions for you. That is the biggest challenge.

Most important advice? Find playwrights your age. Find the people you're going to work with.

The final piece of advice I would give is not to get discouraged. Sometimes it does feel as if you spend a lot of your time justifying your place in the room and some of the resistance comes from the reality that a production can happen without a dramaturg. However, the connections can be stronger, the work can be better and the audience more directly brought into the world of the play. Dramaturgy is an important creative presence in a production and, as a dramaturg, the biggest asset you bring to the room is yourself. The skills can be learned and refined, but an outlook that is dramaturgical – a way to see the world and engage with an audience that is inquisitive, creative, and invested – is a benefit in any room.

Spending time with other dramaturgs is useful, as is finding mentors. Listen to what they have to say. The opportunity to share thoughts and ideas with other theatre artists who take on this challenging and sometimes misunderstood role can help you become a better creative collaborator, and help you continue to learn to dramaturg. With that idea of sharing in mind, the gifted dramaturg Anne Morgan shared her rules for life. These are applicable to all aspects of life, and have been especially relevant in her dramaturgical practice.

The rules are:

1. Don't be an asshole.

    I believe humility is vital to dramaturgy, that what we do is essentially provide a service – to writers, to audiences, to the field.

2. Make yourself useful.

    I began my work in new-play dramaturgy as a Literary Fellow. I made myself useful by tracking script changes, photocopying new pages, and researching glossary terms. As I did this, I was fiercely attuned to the conversations that those around me were having as they dove into the heart of the plays. When the time came, my hard work at the simpler tasks was noticed and I was invited into those same conversations. To this day, finding practical ways to be useful – taking the writer to the grocery store, finding a fan for their room, and so on – has always paid off artistically.

    A recent example: a writer had a guest coming into town, the rehearsal room got extremely tense. I was able to say, "Oh, why don't you and I go get the air mattress I said I'd lend you?" and use that practical reason to leave the tension and talk privately with the writer about how best to approach what was happening in the rehearsal room.

3. Find your people.

    This is perhaps my favorite rule, and its applications are many, but two examples:

    The old saying was that dramaturgs were "the experts in the room." I'm no expert, but I have on many occasions said to a writer, "Oh, you're writing a play about X? Let me help you get a meeting with my sister's friend's cousin's husband who's an expert on the topic." You don't need to be the expert in the room, but by finding your people and cultivating those relationships (both personal and professional) your writer/rehearsal room can still have the necessary expertise.

    Once you've found those relationships, cultivating them can lead to some of the most fruitful collaborations in your career. Or at least it has for me. There is one writer that I've known/been friends with/dramaturged for since we were both 22. I've read (I think) nearly everything he's written. As a result, any conversations about new work, or struggles with an existing writing project, are surrounded by immense context. We both know which points of reference and which methods of working are going to lead in the most successful direction.

4. Read the instructions first.

    I've been fortunate enough to have had a wide variety of drama-turgical experiences – puppet shows, new plays and musicals, plays by Eastern European playwrights working in English for the first time, writer residencies, and so on. I have to constantly remind myself that every situation is different – each writer, each rehearsal room, each theatrical program or institution. Some of the most successful processes I've been a part of have been the ones where working styles and expectations have been articulated at the outset.

A Final Note

The work is important. To dramaturg is a way to strengthen connections among artists. It is a way to speak more directly to audiences. It is a way to engage with material. It is a way to be open and responsive.

Dramaturgy is a way of looking at the world.

ADDITIONAL RESOURCES

The dramaturg should be versed in theatre history, the theatre of her day, performance theory, criticism, culture, and politics. And, plays, she should read a lot of plays. It is not possible to compile a comprehensive list of resources for the dramaturg; it is work that is an ongoing process of discovery and connection.

Consequently, the following list is a starting point for the practice of dramaturgy of performance and text.

Ball, David. *Backwards and Forwards: A Technical Manual for Reading Plays*. Carbondale: Southern Illinois University Press, 1983.

Bly, Mark. *The Production Notebooks: Theatre in Process*. Vols. 1 and 2. 1995. New York: Theatre Communications Group, 2001.

Bogart, Anne. *What's the Story: Essays about Art, Theater, and Storytelling*. New York: Routledge, 2014.

Brown, Lenora Inez. *The Art of Active Dramaturgy: Transforming Critical Thought into Dramatic Action*. Newburyport: Focus Publishing, 2011.

Cardullo, Bert, ed. *What Is Dramaturgy?* New York: Peter Lang Publishing, 2005.

Chemers, Michael Mark. *Ghost Light: An Introductory Handbook for Dramaturgy*. Carbondale: Southern Illinois University Press, 2010.

Hatcher, Jeffrey. *The Art & Craft of Playwriting*. Cincinnati: Story Press, 1996.

Irelan, Scott R., Anne Fletcher, and Julie Felise Dubiner. *The Process of Dramaturgy: A Handbook*. Newburyport: Focus Publishing, 2010.

Jonas, Susan, Geoffrey S. Proehl, and Michael Lupo. *Dramaturgy in American Theatre: A Sourcebook*. New York: Wadsworth, 1996.

Luckhurst, Mary. *Dramaturgy: A Revolution in Theatre*. Cambridge: Cambridge University Press, 2006.

Proehl, Geoffrey S. *Toward a Dramaturgical Sensibility: Landscape and Journey*. Teaneck, NJ: Fairleigh Dickinson University Press, 2011.

Romanska, Madga, ed. *The Routledge Companion to Dramaturgy*. New York: Routledge, 2015.

Theatre Topics 13.1 (Mar. 2003).

Trencsényi, Katalin. *Dramaturgy in the Making*. London: Bloomsbury Methuen Drama, 2015.

INDEX

accuracy 53
action 3, 40, 150
actors 36, 80; career paths for
dramaturgs 188; casebooks 115,
116–17, 121; close attention to
32; clues in the text 26; content
for 64, 65; meetings with 97;
mode of communication 106,
107; notes to 175, 178, 180;
rehearsals 52, 124; social context
24; timing 58; working with
181–5
advice 187–91
aesthetics 28, 50, 51, 105
All for Love (Dryden) 82
ambiguity 94, 96
anachronisms 33–4
Anouilh, Jean 136
Anthony and Cleopatra (Shakespeare)
82
Antigone (Anouilh) 136
attention 58, 72
audiences 8, 131–52; choice
of place 80, 84–7; choice of
time 88–9; communication
with 106, 107; content for 64,
65–6, 104; devised theatre 167;
dramaturg as audience outreach
99–100; "elephant in the room"
73–4, 76–8; engagement with
183; exercises 151–2; holistic
perspective 51, 53; lobby
displays 133–40, 151, 182; play
selection 81, 82; program notes
140–3; questions answered 25–6;
questions asked 32; student
71; study guides 149–51, 152;
talkbacks 143–8, 151–2, 160;
understanding 14, 93; *see also*
outreach
auditions 128
authenticity 33–4, 67; authentic
response 44, 51–2, 54
authority 175, 176

Baker, Annie 82
Ball, David 19
Banksy 73
best practices 187–91
"big picture", seeing the 37–9, 41,
48, 54–5, 89, 133; *see also* holistic
perspective
blocking 28, 30, 38, 57, 62, 179
blogs 121, 128, 132, 151, 186
Bly, Mark 6, 11, 110, 112, 174
Brown, Leonora Inez 11

casebooks 114, 115–23, 124, 129, 142; answers to questions 16, 24, 34; rehearsals 126; schedule of events 127

casting choices 77

Century Cycle (Wilson) 118

character 18, 20, 21, 27, 36, 40; casebooks 119; devised theatre 166; holistic reading of a text 45; new plays 155; script analysis 112; study guides 149, 150; timing 61–2; working with actors 181–2, 183, 184–5

character-name pronunciation 64

characterization 40, 44, 53, 60

Chemers, Michael Mark 4–5, 11, 19

chemistry metaphor 95

Cho, Julia 82

city settings 85–6

collaboration 28, 30, 34, 153–4; with actors 182, 183; with directors 48, 49; dramaturg as collaborator 97–8; flexible thinking 43–4; holistic perspective 54; new plays 156–7, 161, 162, 185; with playwrights 47–8; timing 62

Collins, Billy 6, 112

commentary 65, 66–70; outreach materials 132; program notes 140; reflective 52; staying in the moment 72

communication 35, 61, 95, 105–7; with audience 132–3; casebooks 121–3; with designers and technicians 51; devised theatre 167–8; with directors 48, 125–6; lobby displays 137–9; new plays 154, 159–62; open 174, 185; program notes 143; talkbacks 146–7; *see also* presentation

composition 28, 38, 42; designers 51; directors 52; timing 61

concrete metaphor 95

conduit metaphor 173

conflict 47, 63, 70, 74–5; directors 174–5, 176, 177; talkbacks 159

content 35, 124; casebooks 119–21; delivery 105–6; devised theatre 167–8; gathering 9–10, 95, 101–4, 107, 119–21, 135–7, 138, 142, 146, 158–9, 167–8; lobby displays 135–7, 138; new plays 154, 158–9; pre-production 111; program notes 142; questions answered 16, 26, 53; study guides 149; synthesis of 103, 121, 142; talkbacks 146; when to offer 63–6, 70–1; *see also* information; research

context 14, 20, 42, 79, 100, 185; casebooks 115, 120; devised theatre 163; "elephant in the room" 77; glossaries 119; meaning of 102; questions 16–17, 26; social 24; study guides 149

continuity 52, 53, 124, 125, 129, 164

conventions 20, 22

cooking metaphor 95–6

costume design 38, 57, 125

creativity 7, 89, 169

criticism 60–1

The Crucible (Miller) 88

curation 7–8, 10

deadlines 58–9

Death of a Salesman (Miller) 83

defining the project 9, 95, 96–100, 101, 107; casebooks 116, 119;

devised theatre 167–8; lobby displays 134–5, 138; new plays 157–8; program notes 141–2; study guides 149; talkbacks 144–6
definition of dramaturg 4–7
designers: casebooks 116, 121; clues in the text 26; communication to the audience 80; conversations with 61, 114; holistic perspective 50–1; mode of communication 107; pre-production 113–14; requests for commentary 68; schedule of events 128; social context 24; timing 57, 58
detail 37, 38, 55, 184
devised theatre 146, 163–9, 170, 185, 186–7
digital presentation 105–6, 121–2, 123
directors 36, 48–9; artistic choices 80; career paths for dramaturgs 188; casebooks 116, 121; communication with 106, 125–6; composition 52; content for 64; conversations with 114; devised theatre 168, 187; "elephant in the room" 75; holistic perspective 53; meetings with 97, 98; point of view 42; questions answered 23, 25, 26, 53; questions asked 28–30, 32, 53, 61; requests for commentary 68; schedule of events 127, 128, 129; script suggestions 161; timing 57, 59; working with 174–7, 179
discussion panels 131, 145
displays see lobby displays
Dramatists Guild 162

Dryden, John 82
Dubiner, Julie Felise 11, 110

educational materials 80, 135, 149–51
efficacy 32–3, 34, 43, 48; casebooks 121; mode of communication 107; new plays 154; timing 66, 70
"elephant in the room" 73–8
email 126
An Enemy of the People (Ibsen) 118
Equus (Schaffer) 138
Eugene O'Neill Theatre Center 4
Eurydice (Ruhl) 82, 118
expectations 97, 103, 174; devised theatre 168; directors 176; new plays 156; rehearsals 123
experience, content as 102–3

feedback 29–30, 155, 187
Fences (Wilson) 40–1
Fletcher, Anne 11, 110
flexibility 7, 35, 43–4, 89, 93–4, 174; devised theatre 163–4, 166, 169; effective collaboration 153–4; research 102
The Flick (Baker) 82
flow 53, 63
forest and trees metaphor 37–9, 42, 47, 51, 54, 110, 161; see also holistic perspective
form 18, 20, 35, 44, 124
Fornes, Maria Irene 41
Fuchs, Elinor 112

ghost stories 103
glossaries 101–2, 115, 118–19, 120, 129, 150, 185
goals 49, 50, 99; devised theatre 163; new plays 157, 162; rehearsals 124; talkbacks 160

The Grapes of Wrath (Steinbeck) 139
Greek amphitheatres 86

Hamlet 31
Hedda Gabler (Ibsen) 174
holistic perspective 37–55, 80, 93, 94, 174; audience needs 133; designers, technicians and management 50–1; devised theatre 169; directors 48–9; effective collaboration 153–4; new plays 155, 158, 161; non-production 54; play selection 83; playwrights 46–8; production meetings 49–50; in rehearsal 51–4; script reading 44–6
How I Learned to Drive (Vogel) 45–6
HowlRound 11

Ibsen, Henrik 118, 174
image 18, 27
inaccuracies 36
information: casebooks 115–16; gathering 9–10, 14; program notes 140–3; study guides 149–51; *see also* content
Intimate Apparel (Nottage) 82
Ionesco, Eugène 136
Irelan, Scott 11, 110

"killing your darlings" 161

language 8, 18, 40, 112, 167; *see also* vocabulary
The Language Archive (Cho) 82
Lessing, Gotthold Ephraim 11
listening 58, 83, 114; new plays 154, 155; production meetings 50; rehearsals 52–3, 54; talkbacks 144, 146, 148

Literary Managers and Dramaturgs of the Americas (LMDA) 6, 171
lobby displays 76, 131, 133–40, 182; exercises 151; new plays 186; questions answered 26; questions asked 32; schedule of events 128, 129

management 50–1
marketing 32, 132–3
meaning 22, 40
media 121, 122
"meet the artists" 146
meetings 65, 97, 125; pre-production 113–14; production 49–50; schedule of events 127
mentors 189
metaphors 5, 124, 142, 172–3; dramaturgical process 95–6; reading a text 27, 40, 44
method 9, 95–108; communication of findings 105–7; defining the project 96–100; exercises 107–8; gathering content 101–4; tasks of a dramaturg 110
Miller, Arthur 83, 88
mindset 4, 5–6, 80, 89–90; approach to the material 40; asking questions 14, 28, 34, 35; commentary 67; content offered 66; definition of dramaturg 7; devised theatre 165; dramaturg as practice 93, 94; holistic perspective 37, 38, 43, 46, 54; non-production 54; reading the text 17–18, 21; tasks of a dramaturg 110, 115; timing 56–7, 58, 71, 78; understanding audiences 14
modes of communication 106–7, 122–3, 137–9, 142–3, 168

Morgan, Anne 189
movement 27
Mud (Fornes) 41
music 23, 179; authenticity 33–4;
   holistic perspective 39; working
   with playwrights 46–7

navigational metaphors 114, 172
need-based questions 24
new plays 144, 154–62, 169, 185–6
non-production 54
notes 53, 59, 66, 175, 178, 180; *see*
   also program notes
Nottage, Lynn 82, 145

online resources 102, 105–6, 121
opinion 66–7, 69
Oregon Shakespeare Theatre 4
outreach 26, 76, 80, 131–3;
   deadlines 58; dramaturg as
   audience outreach 99–100;
   exercises 152; play selection 83;
   questions asked 32; *see also* lobby
   displays; program notes; study
   guides; talkbacks

pace 52, 53
panel discussions 131, 145
Parks, Suzan-Lori 82
performance dates 57
place 20, 27, 40; choice of 79–80,
   84–7, 89; holistic reading of a
   text 45; location information in
   glossaries 119, 185
play analysis 113
play selection 79–80, 81–3, 89
playwrights: advocating for 53,
   160, 162, 174; career paths for
   dramaturgs 188; casebooks 115,
   117–18; communication with
   61; devised theatre 164, 166;

"elephant in the room" 75;
   meetings with 97; new plays
   154, 155, 156–62, 185–6; play
   analysis 113; pre-production 111;
   program notes 141; reading the
   text 17–18; rhythm 56; study
   guides 149, 150; women 82;
   working with 30, 46–8, 155
politics 180
posters 139
pre-production 57, 60, 65, 111–15,
   124, 127
presentation 9, 10, 58, 105–7,
   112; casebooks 121–3; devised
   theatre 168; lobby displays
   137–9; program notes 142–3;
   study guides 150; *see also*
   communication
production history 115, 118, 141, 150
production team 36, 89; "elephant
   in the room" 73–5; meetings
   49–50, 97, 113–14, 125, 127;
   questions answered 16, 22–5;
   questions asked 31–2; study
   guides 150; talkbacks 145–6; *see*
   also actors; designers; directors;
   technicians
Proehl, Geoffrey 11
program notes 58, 131, 133, 140–3;
   "elephant in the room" 76, 77;
   questions answered 26; questions
   asked 32; schedule of events 128
project definition *see* defining the
   project
pronunciation 64, 65, 101–2, 118, 119
publicity 80, 132–3, 151

questions 13–35; answering 14–15,
   16–26, 34, 35, 69, 80; asking
   13–15, 26–35, 42, 66, 80, 94,
   187; audiences 25–6, 32; devised

theatre 165; directors 28–30, 53; new plays 158, 161; production team 22–5, 31–2; rehearsals 52, 53, 126; rules for 32–5; talkbacks 146, 147; texts 17–22, 27–8, 33; timing 59–63, 72

read-throughs 52, 58, 65, 123
references 119
reflective commentary 52
rehearsals 26, 123–7, 177–8; devised theatre 163, 168–9; dramaturg as audience advocate 132; "elephant in the room" 75–6; holistic perspective 51–4; questions asked 31; schedule of events 128, 129; timing 57; working with actors 182
relationships 14, 28, 58, 59–60, 174, 175, 190
research 9–10, 101–4, 119–21; dramaturg as researcher 98–9; pre-production 111; production meetings 50; questions 25; scenarios 102; schedule of events 127; see also content
revelation, moments of 178
Rhinocéros (Ionesco) 136
rhythm 40, 41, 44, 52, 53, 56
role 3, 5, 6; active verbs 173; definition of 9, 10; dramaturg as collaborator 97–8; new-play dramaturg 154–5; rehearsals 123–4
Romanska, Magda 11
Ruhl, Sarah 82, 118
Ruined (Nottage) 145
rules: holistic reading of a text 45, 46; for life 189–91; for questions 32–5; questions asked from the text 17, 18, 19, 22, 113

scavenger hunts 129–30
schedules 57–9, 62, 70–1, 72, 78, 127–9, 165
school groups 149, 150
scripts: devised theatre 163, 164, 165; directors' suggestions 161; holistic reading of 44–6; new plays 155, 158; play selection 82; practice reading 170; questions answered 16, 17–22; rehearsals 124; schedule of events 127, 128; script analysis 18, 19, 22, 31–2, 40, 111–13, 114, 126; script development 47; see also texts
season planning 81
The Second Shepherds' Play (Wakefield Cycle) 85
selection of play 79–80, 81–3, 89
self-reflection 9
sexual scenes 74–5
Shaffer, Peter 138
Shakespeare, William 82, 99
Smith, Anna Deavere 85
sound design 39
space 21, 85
staged readings 156
story 18, 19, 22, 27, 133; devised theatre 163, 166; holistic reading of a text 45, 46; new plays 155
structure 18, 19–20, 22; devised theatre 164; holistic reading of a text 45, 46; new plays 155; rhythm 56; transitions 184
study guides 58, 131, 133, 149–51, 152
style 18, 27, 44, 45, 63, 150
synthesis of content 103, 121, 142

talkbacks 131, 133, 143–8; "elephant in the room" 76, 77; exercises 151–2; new plays 159–60; prompts for 64;

questions answered 26; schedule of events 129

tasks of a dramaturg 5, 10, 12, 109–10; casebooks 115–23; lobby displays 133–40; pre-production 111–15; program notes 140–3; rehearsals 123–7; study guides 149–51; talkbacks 143–8

technicians 24, 50–1, 58

texts: devised theatre 164, 168; holistic reading of 44–6; questions answered 17–22, 33; questions asked 27–8, 33; *see also* scripts

theatres 84, 86

themes 18, 40, 124, 142, 149

time 18, 20, 21, 27, 40, 173–4; casebooks 120; choice of 79–80, 87–9; holistic reading of a text 45–6

timing 56–78, 80, 174; asking a question 59–63; devised theatre 165–6, 169; "elephant in the room" 73–8; lobby displays 136; new plays 155, 157, 158; rehearsals 125; schedule of events 127–9; sharing of content 71; staying in the moment 71–2; talkbacks 147–8; when to offer commentary 66–70; when to offer content 63–6, 70–1

Topdog/Underdog (Parks) 82

translation 96–7

truth 33–4, 40

Twilight: Los Angeles 1992 (Smith) 85

usage 43

verb, dramaturg as a 3–11, 93–4, 110

vision 44, 53; commentary 67; directors 28, 29, 48–9; new plays 159

visual imagery 65, 101; casebooks 115; devised theatre 163, 165, 167; program notes 143

visual landscape 42, 85, 89, 111

vocabulary 20, 113, 114; devised theatre 167; glossaries 119; new plays 159; program notes 142; script analysis 44; *see also* language

Vogel, Paula 45

Wakefield Cycle 85

way of seeing, dramaturgy as a 153, 172

websites 132

Williams, Tennessee 118

Wilson, August 40–1, 118

witnessing 179–80

women playwrights 82